THE UNKNOWN RIGVEDA'S AND ATHENIAN'S

PANIKKAR'S CHRISTOLOGICAL PRAYāṇA 2

CHERIYAN MENACHERRY

Contents

Preface

The Unknown of the Rigveda and the Athenians: Panikkar's Christological prayāṇa 2 is the Indian Edition of the book already published in Europe.[1]

The Mediating Mystery, CHRIST, the *Deo ignoto*, present in all religions, even if unknown, the one who even makes religion possible and transcends it, is the *religatio* between God and the world. Religions can meet in the very source. All religions have different symbols for CHRIST, the one Mediator. The Rigvedic expression 'what God' (*kasmai devāya*) (RV 10, 121, 1-9) is not a question but the naming of the unknown Mediator, the cosmotheandric principle, the *prajāpati* (RV 10, 121, 10) The Athenians had an altar to the unknown god, *Agnostos Theos*. Recognising that the altar was for the unknown Mediator of the Athenians, Paul preached Christ on the Areopagus (Acts 17:22 ff.).

Panikkar's Christological Prayāṇa series, the result of the revision of my book Christ: *The Mystery in History: A Critical Study on the Christology of Raymond* Panikkar (1996),[2] presents Raymond Panikkar's insights into understanding the mystery of Christ from the perspective of Hinduism. *The Unknown of the Rigveda and the Athenians*, the second book in the series, is more concerned with Panikkar's explanation of the principle of the mediation of an absolute Brahman with the world by analysing the *Brahmasutra*. *The* authors of the Hindu scriptures, e.g., the *Brahmasutras* and their commentators, were not explicitly thinking of CHRIST when they wrote about *Īśvara*. Similarly, the Christ in whom Christians believe cannot be equated with *Īśvara*. However, if one analyses the *sensus plenior*, a broader sense of the philosophical and theological texts of humanity, one arrives at the *res significata*, the intention of the *advaitic Īśvara*, which leads to the philosophical possibility of a Christ. If the goal of Hinduism is CHRIST and Christianity, then it is not the present form of Christianity or the present image of CHRIST that Christianity has. But it is a perfect Christianity that strives to embrace the fullness of Christ. When Hinduism and Christianity come to understand the full CHRIST as cosmotheandric reality through the 'unknown Christ of Hinduism', then 'ecumenical Christophany' is achieved.

Prof. Dr. Cheriyan Menacherry CMI,

Bisingen, Germany

18th February 2025, on the feast of St. Kuriakose Elias Chavara

[1] Menacherry, Cheriyan. *Rigveda's and Athenians' Unknown.: Panikkar's Christological prayāṇa 2*, Chisinau, Moldova: Blessed Hope Publishing, 2022.

[2] Menacherry, Cheriyan. *Christ: The Mystery in History: A Critical Study on the Christology of Raymond Panikkar*. Peter Lang Publ Inc. (June 1996).

Sanskrit Glossary

Advaita. Non-duality, a non-dualistic philosophical view of reality, not to be confounded with monism

advitīyam. Lit. 'not having a second'

aham. I, the absolute I

ākāśa. Air, sky, space, ether, vacuity (emptiness), atmosphere, thefifth of the primordial elements (*mahābhūtāni:* earth, water, fire,air, ether) which is the element of sound. It is all-penetratingand infinite, hence frequently identified with *Brahman*

asya. 'of this' (Gen.)

ānanda. Joy, bliss, beatitude

anubhava. Direct experience, knowledge derived from immediate spiritualinsight

ātman. the Self

avatāra. 'decent', incarnation of Vishnu in animal or human form

avidyā. Ignorance

bhagavān. 'The blessed One', the Lord

bhāsya. Commentary

byāṣyakāra. Commentator

brahman. The Absolute, the World-ground

cit. Consciousness

darśana. Vision, world-view, philosophical system

dharma. Universal cosmic law, order, religion

dharmakāya. Lit. 'body of dharma or truth'. One of the three aspects which together constitute the Mahāyāna Buddhist conception of Tripple Body (*Trikāya: dharmakāya, nirmānakāya* or body of transformation and *Sambhogakāya* or Body of Bliss). The *dharmakāya* refers to the Buddha as the absolute, formless, ineffable realitywhich underlies all phenomena.[1]

dushṭa. Wicked

dvaita. Duality, dualism as philosophical system

eka. One, frequently *tat ekam*, the One as the origin of everything,later identified with *Brahman*

ekatva. Oneness

guṇa. Quality, property, etc. In the *Sāṁkhya* system the three'qualities' or fundamental constituents of *prakṛti* (nature), viz., *sattva* (modality of luminosity and intelligence), *rajas* (modality of motor energy and mental activity), *tamas* (modality of staticinertia and psychic obscurity)_[2]

idam. 'this', the World

iṣtadevatā. The deity proper to a person or a group for worship and meditation; the chosen or proper deity

Īśvara. The Lord, God

janmādi. Origin etc.

jīva. The individual soul

jñāna. Knowledge, higher wisdom

ka. Interrogative pronoun 'who' one of the names of *prajāpati*

kali. The last and most degenerate of the four cosmic periods (*yuga*). We are now living in the *kaliyuga.*

Kālī. A goddess (other names: Satī, Pārvatī, Durga, Umā, Bhavāni), the *śakti* of Śiva. She also symbolizes eternal time and hence she both gives and destroys it._[3]

kalki. The tenth *avatāra* of Vishnu at the end of the *kali Yuga* ('dark age'). He will destroy a world sunk in corruption. After this destruction, Vishnu will rebuild the world anew._[4]

karma. Act, action, accumulated result of past actions

Kṛṣna. Avatāra of *viṣṇu* (lit. 'the black one') and one of the most popular of the Gods. He does not occur in the Veda, but it is he who reveals the BG

mahātmā. 'Great soul'; title of a sage or a saint

mahāvākya. The (traditionally four) Great Utterances of the Upaniṣads concerning *ātman* and *brahman*. Plural: *mahāvākyāni* simplified to *mahāvākyās*

mantra. Prayer, sacred formula, holy word, a Vedic text or verse

māyā. Divine power, power of illusion, World-illusion

mīmāṁsa. One of the six classical systems dealing mainly with thefoundations of and the rules for interpreting Vedic texts. *Pūrvamīmāmsa* deals with the ritual interpretation of the Veda. *Uttaramīmāmsa* or *Vedānta* gives a philosophical or spiritualinterpretation.

mokṣa. Liberation, salvation

nāma-rūpa. Name and form, the constituents of the reality World

Nārāyaṇa. The 'son of Man' (*nara*) i.e., of the original *puruṣa*; a namefor God in the form of Viṣṇu or Kṛṣṇa.

neti neti. 'not so, not so' referring to the ultimate reality or theSelf which can be expressed only negatively

nirguṇa. (*Brahman*) without attributes

nirvāṇa. Extinction, liberation (mainly in Buddhism)

om. The sacred syllable, consisting of the three letters A-U-M. It means also 'yes', 'so be it'.

prakṛti. Nature, primary matter; in Sāṁkhya one of the two fundamentalprinciples of the universe (*puruṣa* and *prakṛti*)

pāramārthika. The ultimate level, the ultimately real

paramātman. The supreme *ātman*, God; the term used to distinguish theuniversal from the individual *ātman*

prajāpati. 'The Lord of creatures,' the primordial God, Father of theGods and of all beings. His position is central in the Brāhmaṇa.

pramāṇa. Means of valid knowledge

prayāṇa. Journey, progress

puruṣa. Original, archetypal Man, Person

Rāma. *Avatāra* of Viṣṇu and one of the most popular Hindu Gods, themodel of righteousness.

ṛṣi. Sage, seer (of the Veda)

śabda. Sound, word. One aspect of *Brahman* as the revealed, manifestedone, *śabda-brahman*

saccidānanda. *Brahman* as Being (*sat*), Consciousness (*cit*) and Bliss(*ānanda*)

saguṇa. (*Brahman*) endowed with qualities. In Vedānta *saguṇa brahman* is equivalent of *īśvara*, the Lord.

śakti. Divine power, creative energy of the God, conceived in female form

sa,mhāra. Dissolution, destruction (of the World at the end of a cosmic period)

saṃsāra. Worldly existence, transmigration

saṃskāra. 'Sacrament', rites sanctifying the different stages of human life

sanātana dharma. 'Eternal religion', self-designation of Hinduism

sat. Being

Śvetaketu. Son of Gautama, a famous disciple of Uddālaka in CU to whom the highest teaching (*tattavamasi*) is imparted.

Śiva. The Auspicious One; in the Veda it is Rudra who, since the *Śvetāśvatara Upanishad* is known as Śiva, one of the most important Gods of the Hindu tradition

sṛṣṭi. Creation, emanation

śruti. 'That which has been heard', revelation of the Vedas, authoritative Scriptures of Hinduism

śūnyatā. Void, absolute emptiness as the ultimate reality in Buddhism

sūtra. Lit. 'thread', short aphorism

tad. Demonstrative pronoun: that. Contrary to *idam* (this), it refers to *Brahman.* When occuring alone, it points to the ultimate reality without naming it. *tat ekam:* the One, that One

upamāna. Comparison, one of the 'means of knowledge' (*pramāṇa*)

vāc. The Word, speech, a sacred principle in the Veda

Vaiṣṇava. The cult of Viṣṇu, and a term for a follower of the cult. Vaiṣṇava is one of the three great divisions of modern Hinduism, the other two being the Śaiva and Śākta._[5]

veda. Lit. knowledge; the sacred knowledge incorporated in the Veda as the whole body of 'Sacred Scriptures'. In the narrow sense 'Veda' refers only to the Samhitās (*Rigveda, Yajurveda, Samaveda, Atharvaveda*); in the broader sense *brāhmaṇas, Aranyakas* and *Upanishads* are included. In the plural it refers to the four Vedas.

vedānta. Lit. 'end of the Veda,' i.e., the *Upanishads* as the culmination of Vedic wisdom. In the sense of *Uttaramīmāmsā* or *Vedāntavāda*, one system of Indian philosophy (*advaita Vedānta, dvaita Vedānta* etc.) based on the *Upanishads* and teaching a spiritual interpretation of the Vedas

viśiṣṭādvaita. Doctrine of 'qualified non-dualism', represented by Rāmānuja

Viṣṇu. The important God in Hinduism, already occurring in the Veda; his name means something like 'the all penetrating.' He is related to the sun. Later he becomes the second of the *trimūrti*, the preserver, and he is mainly worshipped in his *avatāras.*

vyāvahārika. Worldly reality, relative level

[1] E.J. Coleman, in *Abingdon Dictionary of Living Religions*, Gen. Ed., Keith Crim, (Tennessee: Abingdon, 1981), pp. 222, 768-769.

[2] Margaret and James Stutley, , *A Dictionary of Hinduism: Its Mythology, Folklore and Development* 1500 B.C.-A.D. 1500 (Bombay: Allied Publishers, 1977), pp. 243-244.

[3] Stutley, *A Dictionary of Hinduism:...* (1977), pp. 137-138.

[4] Vassilis G. Vitsaxis, *Hindu Epics, Myths and Legends in Popular Illustrations*, (Oxford: Oxford University Press, 1977), p. 63.

[5]Stutley, , *A Dictionary of Hinduism:...* (1977), p. 317.

ONE

1 MEETING IN THE CAUSE OF RELIGIONS

Since the task is to find a fundamental meeting of the world's religions, Panikkar is not concerned with a purely ideological agreement[1] through doctrinal comparisons[2] or such methods. The agreements reached through social, legal or even individual encounters are necessary but not sufficient.[3] Any progress towards unity thus achieved remains minor in the face of the fundamental differences between religions. The emphasis must be on meeting at the centre.[4] The search is for the original source of all religions. In that source all can perhaps meet, even transcending the basic discrepancies. We need to go on deeper and deeper till we "experience the same `currents'" in different religions.[5] This will allow us to dig out a common foundation for meeting together.[6] There is no doubt that the religions, for example Hinduism and Christianity, can meet in the ultimate mystery, the transcendent God, as "God is working inside both religions and transcends them."[7]

A. Religions Meet in Their Source

Light is the source of the differing colours that come through the prism. There is no doubt that the colours of the spectrum can meet in their source. But what is the mystery behind the ability for refraction and dispersion in the light [God]? Panikkar's analogy of the refraction of light bears some resemblance to St. Gregory of Nazianzus' analogy of light to explain the Trinitarian mystery: "...there is one mingling of light, as if in three suns joined to each other. When we look at the Godhead, or the First Cause, or the Monarchy, that which we perceive is One; but when we look at the Persons in whom the Godhead resides,...there are Three whom we worship."[8] Both Christianity and Hinduism can go further than accepting God as the common foundation for meeting together. There is the mediating mystery in God that enables Him to be in communion with the universe and *vice versa*. This mystery is the source of religion. "Panikkar puts the point concisely, `Religions meet where religions take their source'".[9] "In other words, Christianity and Hinduism meet in a common endeavour, which has the same starting point and the same `ontic' goal."[10] Both Hinduism and Christianity have experienced this mediating mystery in God. There is "the presence of the one Mystery...in both traditions."[11] Finding this one link, one mediator between God and the world, between the one and the many is crucial.[12] While commenting on *Brahma Sūtra* I.1.2, Panikkar says that it aims to find out the under-lying, or above-dwelling reality which both traditions are talking about.[13] In this "deepest recess of reality--in what Christian tradition calls the Mystery"[14] the two religions can meet.

B. The Mediating Mystery: Transcendent and Immanent.

There is a longing in religions to come to union. This longed-for union must not be postulated as to be realised in the transcendent "where differences matter no longer where we are no longer in and of this World--but here in this World where we are fellow-pilgrims, where we commune in our humanness, in the *samsāric* adventure, in our historical situation".[15] The vision for a union of religions must be while accepting "our *karma* and our *siddhis*, our limitations as well as our gifts. We need to swim in the stream of history without ceasing to fly in the air (*ākāśa*) of the timeless. We need incarnation as much as transcendence, and we should take our *iṣtadevatā*, the manifestation for us of the Divine, as a real symbol, something more than a mere sign."[16]

There is hope that the encounter is already taking place in this world, in present human history. Hinduism would say "...either we meet as sister religions striving towards the same end, or we meet by sacrificing our individual ways and coalescing in the mysterious divine ground of our Origin and End."[17] The suggestion from Hinduism may be perhaps we have already met before the starting of history, all rivers have the same source, for instance the clouds. And there is also the future possibility of merging at the end of history, all rivers flow to the sea.[18] That means if we wish union to happen within history then it is by being absorbed "into one of the many Hindu branches."[19] In short, "the meeting point cannot be only a transcendent platform, divine ground, a disincarnated place, as it were."[20] We need a concrete meeting-place, which is more than just an idea or a concept and also more than just humanity with its material needs.[21]

The transcendent and historical aspect of union of the religions is inspired by the very nature of the divine mediating mystery, which is not a purely transcendent divine reality, in which all people worship or recognize, in their different ways, one and the same transcendent God. "It is equally immanent and `this-worldly`; it is also *sagunic* in character and even possesses an historical dynamism."[22] Śaṅkara recognized two forms of *Brahman* (Cf. BU II, 3, 1; Mait U VI, 3.): The one, without attributes and absolutely unrelated, the other with attributes and `cause` of the world. Nonetheless Śaṅkara, according to `Scripture` (BS III, 3,39), stresses the unity of the twofold *Brahman*.[23]

The deeper awareness of the `mediating principle`, *Īśvara*, comes in Hindu philosophy when the relation between God and the world is dealt with.[24] The case of CHRIST is not very different from this situation. Everything "is in him, and we, with all our striving and all our actions, are of him, in him, come from him and go to him."[25] In both Christian and Hindu traditions there is the experience of the mystery participating in transcendence and immanence, other-worldly and this-worldly.

C. CHRIST: the Only Mediator in the Trinity

In the Trinity and in the `Paratrinitarian' experiences, only CHRIST participates in both the Divine, and the cosmic aspects. There "is only one link, one mediator between God and the rest. That is Christ,...It is Christ who leads every man to God; there is no other way but through him."[26] He is the "only mediator between creation and the Father (I Tim 2:5)."[27] In explaining about the only Mediator Panikkar reinterprets the trinitarian mystery, especially that of Greek patristic tradition and the Latin Bonaventurian scholastic.[28] He then enters into the deep intuitions of Hinduism and Buddhism, which comes from a different universe of discourse than the Greek,[29] hoping to help to penetrate further the trinitarian mystery.

Entering into the thinking pattern of *Vedanta* is more conducive to enter deep into the mystery of Trinity. When Panikkar employs *advaita* in Vedanta for understanding the relations in the Trinity, he does not mean, *advaita* Vedanta of Śaṅkaracharya, the ultimate experience of the essential non-separability of the Self (*ātman*) and 'God' (*brahman*).[30] Panikkar depends mainly on *Vedanta's* (the Upanishads, the *Brahma-Sūtra* and the Bhagavad Gita), especially the Upanishad's *advaita*. "Advaita (as differentiated from Advaita Vedānta) would be the fundamental principle of nondualism (*a-dvaita*: nonduality), devoid of its connections with the rest of the Vedāntic philosophical garb."[31]

The *advaita* helps not only to express suitably the God-World `relation', but it is also a precious aid in elucidating the intra-trinitarian problem.[32] Dr. Alan Watts is of the opinion that to explain Trinity one must enter into the thinking pattern of Vedanta. He commented that Panikkar had made the distinction between non-dualism and monism. For, the Christian theologians

...confused *tat-tvam asi*, or the Atman is Brahman, with monism. `Well, if we're all one glob,' they say, `there can't be any love, because love implies relationship.'...If you believe in the Trinity, you can also stretch your mind...to the position of the Vedanta. Non-dualism is a funny word, because it's used instead of oneness; but the opposite of oneness is either none or many. We need a word that expresses something which has no opposite, and that nevertheless doesn't oppose opposition. Now we can't express three dimensions on a two-dimensional surface, but we can employ a convention which is a line with a slant to a vanishing point.[33]

With the reinterpretation of *advaita* Panikkar points out that only CHRIST (the Son), and neither the Father nor the Holy Spirit, has the possibility for the mediating function. The unity of religions can be achieved by maximum ecumenism, by finding similarity in the highest religious experiences. He draws inspiration also from the <u>mahāvakyas</u>: <u>*Ekamevam advitīyam*</u>, One alone without a second; *Neti, neti*, not so, not so. *Atman Brahman*, the self and ground of each thing is God; *Aham Brahmāsmi*, I am *Brahman*; *Tattvamasi*, That art Thou.[34] And above all the BS I,1,2. *Janmādasya yataḥ*, whence the origin *et cetera* of this.

D. Father, the Transcendent Absolute, as *Brahman*

Panikkar analyzes the roles of the Father and the Spirit in the light of the insights of Buddhism and *Advaita*. As the Father can be approached only apophatically (*Neti, neti*, Not So, Not So), He is not the Mediator.

i.   Father, the Absolute, the Only God, *o theós*

Father and *Brahman* both signify the divine transcendence.[35] In all religious traditions the Absolute is un-nameable, *a-nāma*, an-onymous. In the Christian tradition "this Absolute has a definite designation: `The Father of our Lord Jesus Christ'."[36] The Father in Himself has no name. Maximus the Confessor says: "The name of God and Father, which is essentially subsistent, is his Logos."[37] The Father is the Absolute, the only God, *o theós*. There are not three Gods: "The Trinity is not tri-theism."[38] Significantly, the first trinitarian *formulae* do not speak of the Father, the Son and the Spirit, but of the God, the Christ and the Spirit. Panikkar is following the approach of the Eastern Fathers, "which is centered on God the Father, God means the Father; Son and Holy Spirit are conceived as participating in His divinity."[39] Neither the Son nor the Spirit is God, but, precisely, the Son of God and the Spirit of God, equal to the One God (*o theós*) as God (*theós*).[40] "One cannot say of the Son that he is equal to the Father any more than one can say that he is different." Panikkar may be alluding to "the same Spirit,...the same Lord and...the same God." (1 Cor 12:4-6); and also to "There is...one Spirit...one Lord...one God and Father of us all, who is above all and through all and in all." (Eph 4:4-6).[41] The Nicene Creed, the Greek Fathers and even Tertullian, affirm that the substratum of the Divinity resides in the Father.[42]

i. **The Father is *Not***

The Father begets the Son. By the divine generation He gives Himself fully to the Son. That means, what the Son is, is the Father, i.e., the Son is the *is* of the Father. Father, *qua* Father, separately, in itself, *is not*. To the question: what is Father? We must reply: it is Son. To know the Son *qua* Son is to realise the Father also; to know Being as such implies to have transcended it in a *non-ontical* way.[43] As a result, "the Absolute, the Father, *is not*." [44] It seems in saying that the Father is not--since the `*is not*' in italics--, Panikkar is not contradicting the Fourth Lateran General Council statement: "Nor can we say that in generating, the Father transferred His substance to the Son, as though He gave it to the Son in such a way as not to retain it for Himself, for so He would have ceased to be substance."[45] Panikkar explains, the Father has no *ex-sistence*, not even that of Being. In the generation of the Son he has, so to speak, given everything. In the Father the apophasis (the *kenosis* or emptying) of Being is real and total. This is "`the Cross in the Trinity' i.e. the integral immolation of God, of which the Cross of Christ and his immolation are only the images and revelations."[46]

iii. **The Father is Non-self, No Person**

The Father is the source of Being, the absolute and ultimate *I*.[47] At the same time, it is inadequate to say that the Father is the unique and absolute *I* without reference to a *thou*, the Son. The Father in Himself, is not even an *I*: He affirms Himself only through the Son in the Spirit. He does not affirm Himself, He affirms. Therefore, no statement about the Trinity is true if taken in isolation from the other equally constitutive relations.[48]

Nothing can be said of the Father `in Himself', of the `self' of the Father, for, in begetting the Son He gives up everything, even the possibility of being expressed in a name that would speak of Him and Him alone, outside any reference to the generation of the Son.[49] In his apophatic statements concerning the Father, Panikkar may be following Clement of Alexandria. According to the latter, one can recognize God through the Logos, because the Father cannot be named, He is Unknown. He is infinite, indivisible and without any dimension. And, therefore He is without form and name: "No one can rightly express Him wholly. For on account of His greatness He is ranked as the All, and is the Father of the universe. Nor are any parts to be predicated of Him. For the One is indivisible; wherefore also it is infinite, not considered with reference to its being with-out dimensions, and not having a limit. And, therefore, it is without form and name."[50] And if we name Him, "we do not do so properly .... It remains that we understand then the Unknown by divine grace and by the Word alone that proceeds from Him."[51] Panikkar finds here, in this essential outgoing movement of the `person' of the Father, in this *kenosis* of Being at its very source, that the Buddhist experience of *nirvāṇa* and *sūnyatā* (emptiness) can be situated. One is led onwards towards the `absolute goal' and, at the end, "one finds nothing, because there is nothing, not even Being. `God created out of nothing'...i.e. out of himself (*a Deo*)--a Buddhist will say."[52]

According to the Upaniṣads *Brahman* is certainly not self-consciousness (which is the *ātman* realised). Similarly, one can say: 'What the Father knows is the Son.' Often this is falsely understood: "...since the Son is not the accusative, the object of the Father's knowledge. He could then not be a person." Instead of saying `what, whom' (*quod, quem*, in the accusative) it is better to say `Who' (*quod, quis* in the nominative), even though, grammatically, this is incorrect. `Who the Father knows is the Son.' "The Son is not an object, he is the knowledge of the Father, since he is the Being, the *asti*, the *esti* of the Father. The `identity' is total and the `alterity' equally total, infinite and absolute: *alius* <u>non</u>*aliud*, as the scholastics used to say."[53]

iv. The Father is Not Logos but Silence

As the Father is total silence, the approach to the Father is through silence.

Buddhism seems to be expressing the spirituality of the Father. Buddhism stresses that "to speak of the ultimate mystery makes *non-sense*, that to manipulate the Supreme, even with our intelligence, is a blasphemy and that silence is the base and source of all speech, all thought and all being."[54] Panikkar is near to the idea of Ignatius of Antioch, who has suggested that the Word proceeds from silence: "...there is one God, who manifested Himself through His Son, Jesus Christ, who is His Word proceeding from silence, and who was in all respects pleasing to Him that sent Him."[55] Jesus is the mouth of the Father who is silence, Jesus Christ "is the mouth which cannot lie, by which the Father has spoken truly."[56]

Any attempt to *speak* about the Father, according to Panikkar, involves almost a contradiction in terms, for every word about the Father can only refer to the one of whom the Father is Father, that is, to the Word, to the Son. It is necessary to be silent.[57] Only "in the interior cell where the logos is silent can the Father be adored in spirit and truth."[58] The most diverse religious traditions teach that

God is Silence.[59] "God is Silence total and absolute, the silence of Being--and not only the being of silence. His word who completely expresses and consumes Him, is the Son. The *Father has* no being[,] the Son is his being. The source of being is not being. If it were, how could it be its source? *'Fons et origo totius divinitatis,'*--source and origin of the whole divinity."[60]

v) Father: The Absolute Goal, but Not the Way

Brahman is the goal, <u>lakṣya</u> (Mund U. II,2,3-4.).[61] "That from which truly all beings are born, by which...they live and into which they all return:..(TU III, 1)."[62] "'From Bliss--*ā<u>nanda</u>*--alone, these beings originate, being originated, by Bliss do they live, unto Bliss do they return' (TU III,6.). *Brahman* is essentially: omniscient cause, eternally pure, intelligent and free."[63]

There can only be an apophatic approach to the Father. "Devotion to the Father meets an apophatism of Being; it is a movement towards...no place, a prayer which is always open towards...the infinite horizon which, like a mirage, always appears in the distance because it is no-where."[64] Everything comes out of the Father of Lights, but everything goes to Him. At the same time, one cannot reach him any more than a meteor can reach the sun without being evaporated and thus disappearing before getting there. Still, "it is equally impossible to avoid being carried along in the current which draws everything towards Him, the Father. One can be united *with* the Son or one may be *in* the Spirit but one can never *be* the Father, because the Father *is not*. One can never reach him because there is no 'end' to attain. And yet all things tend to Him as their ultimate goal."[65]

One goes to the Father only through the Son. To go *directly to* the Father does not even make sense. The so-called way to the Father is non-way, non-thought, non-being.[66] One can participate in the sonship because the Father causes the Sonship. "No one can come to me, if the Father who sent me does not draw him." (Jn 6:44). If one goes to the Son, it is because one already participates in his sonship. The Father has already included the human person in the Sonship of His Son.[67] The Father calls His Son and it is through this calling that the whole creation is called.[68] "Even the Son only knows the Father in being known by Him: `You are my Son; today I have begotten you', `*Aham asmi*', `*ego eimi o eimi*', `I am who I am.` Creation is the echo of that divine primordial cry."[69]

E. The Spirit: The Divine Immanence, not the Mediator

If Father and *Brahman* signify the divine transcendence,[70] both Spirit and *Atman* reveal the divine immanence, the revelation of the Immanent God.[71] This immanence is not simply a negative transcendence, it "signifies the ultimate inner-ness of every being, the final foundation, the *Ground* of Being as well as of beings."[72]

i. The Spirit: The Divine Dynamism Consummated

Everything that the Father *is*, He transmits to the Son. Everything that the Son *receives* he *gives* to the Father in return. This gift (of the Father, in the final analysis) is the Spirit."[73] The process is to the Father through the Son; and the culmination of it is in the Spirit (Jn 14:17, 26; 15:26; 16:14.).[74] If the Father and the Son are not *two*, they are not one either: the Spirit both unites and distinguishes them. "He is the bond of unity; the *we* in between, or rather within."[75] In describing the Holy Spirit as "we" and the Son "thou" Panikkar sounds similar to idea of Heribert Mühlen who finds the communitarian dimension in the Trinity: I (*Ich*), thou (*du*) and *we* (wir): "Ich" the Father, "Du" the Son and "Wir" the Holy Spirit.[76] The Father, the ultimate I, generates the Son as His thou. The Son manifests the Father. The Spirit is personified love of the Father and the reciprocal gift of the Son. The Spirit is also the nonduality (*advaita*) of the Father and Son. Advaitic mystery in the Trinity shows that there are not three distinct beings.[77] The internal Trinitarian love is *advaitic*: As the only I the Father loves himself, "discovers his nonduality (which is the Spirit) in the (him)self which is the Thou (the Son)." The Trinity can help the *advaita* to "show that nondualism can have room for Love--understood precisely as the inner movement of this `One without a second' (*ekam eva advitīyam*) ...."[78]

If the Father is source and origin of the whole divinity,[79] and if the Son *is* God from the Father[80], as the Greek Church Fathers say, developing the image, the River who flows from the Source, "then the Spirit is, as it were, the End, the limitless Ocean where the flux of divine life is completed, rests and is consummated ...."[81] The Father is Source, the Son is Being, the *Thou*, "and the Spirit, Return to Being (or Ocean of Being), the *we*. Paul's trinitarian formulation of God `above all, *through* all and *in* all' (Eph. 4:6) gives us the clue."[82]

a. *Brahman, Atman*: I and Thou advaitic experience

It is to the Spirit that most of the Upaniṣadic assertions about the Absolute point refer.[83] The Spirit is but the *ātman* of the Upanishads, which is said to be identical with *brahman*.[84] But it is not said that *brahman* is *ātman*.[85] In the `*ātman* is *brahman*', the *is* has a peculiar character. [86] For instance, in the statements `John *is* good' and `five is more than three,' the *is* has not the same meaning, the meaning of *is* depends on the subject and the predicate it unites.[87]

So also, the "meaning of the verb *is* here is built into the *ātman* which is *brahman* and expresses only the ultimate identity between them."[88] The "is" of "God is" depends on the very nature of God and thus cannot be compared with any other thing that is. The "is" of the *ātman*, that is *brahman*, is again *sui generis* and depends on the specific nature of *ātman*. It is not a logical, but an *ātman* identity.[89] The *brahman* is my *ātman*. The realization of the *ātman* leads us to discover its identity with *brahman*, that is, to discover its ultimate immanence leads to its recognition as the absolute transcendence.[90] "The ātman is that which holds the human person together in unity and guides the individual selves as their Lord."[91] The *Kauśītāki Upaniṣad* says: "Just as a razor might be hidden in a razor-case or as fire in the fireplace, even so, this self of intelligence has entered this bodily self, up to the very hairs and nails. On that self these other selves depend as upon a chief his own (men) or as his own (men) are of service to a chief, even so these other selves are of service to that self of (intelligence)." (Kaus U IV, 20).[92] *Śvetāśvatara Upaniṣad* states: "Subtler than even the subtlest and greater than the greatest, the Atman is concealed in the heart of the creature." (SU III, 20). St Paul wrote: "Do you not know that you are God's temple and that God's Spirit dwells in you?" (I Cor 3:16). This *ātman* is the supreme Person, *uttama puruṣa* (Cf. CU VIII, 12, 3 (§ VI 6)).[93] Panikkar compares the immanence of *ātman*, the supreme Person, in a human being with drop of water and ocean: "The (water contained in the) drop is the ocean once it has reached the ocean, but the ocean is not the drop."[94]

The union of the Father and the Spirit is Christian doctrine. The transcendent God and the immanent Spirit are in perfect union. This identity has to be existentially recognized by the attainment of the final realization. The *end* of every individual is the recognition that this *ātman* is identical with *brahman*.[95]

The person is only in relationship with the I; thou art in relationship with the I which is love. This experience is expressed by *Chāndogya Upaniṣad* as *Tat tvam asi* (CU VI, 8, 7sq.).

The essence of the person is relationship; my person is nothing but a relation with the I. Properly speaking, the place of my personality is within the single Thou of the unique I. But my person is also related to others, it touches, so to speak, the shores of the reality of other people. My person is also related to my beloved whom I call thou, and this I-thou relationship makes us emerge from nothingness by the power of the life-giving Spirit who is Love. Thus, we enter more and more into the Thou of ultimate I who is not different from God Himself. This is the ultimate level of human love and likewise the very condition of its possibility: when the Spirit responds through us to God. Here the personality reaches maturity, which is pure transparency .... *Tat tvam asi* (CU VI, 8, 7sq.).[96]

To the verse (VI-viii-7) of *Chāndogya Upaniṣad*: "That is the Atman. That thou art, O Śvetaketu", Panikkar gives the following explanation: "A *Thou* you are, Śvetaketu! We are in as far as we are the *Thou*, the *tvam* of the One." [97] "`In the beginning was the Logos' the *New* Testament affirms. `At the end will be the *ātman*' adds the wisdom of this *cosmic* Testament."[98]

ii. Faith in the Spirit: The Ultimate Silence

The approach to the Spirit is not in 'personal' structures. It does not consist in the discovery of Someone, and even less in dialogue with him. It consists rather in the consciousness that one is not found outside reality; in the realisation that one is, so to speak, included in it; that one is already *there*, that one is known to and loved by it. There is a kind of total passivity. There is no *me* to save. The spirituality of the Spirit "is the way of silence--the silence of words no doubt but also that of desires, that of action, the silence, finally, of being, of wishing to be, the total silence of the will to be .... Faith in the Spirit cannot be formulated; it too is silent."[99]

iii. Praying: not to or through, but in the Spirit

There is no question of having personal relations with the Spirit. Through the Spirit one cannot reach the Transcendent, the Other. One cannot pray *to* the Spirit as an isolated term of our prayer. What one can have is a non-relational union with the Spirit. We can pray *in* the Spirit, by addressing the Father through the Son. It is the Spirit who prays in us. When one embarks on "the way of the Spirit, one can only reach the extraontic foundation of everything."[100]

The Mediator's role is to relate the attraction of the transcendent Father and the desire for communion in the immanent Spirit. "Man finds himself, as it were, under the arc which stretches between the transcendent God and the immanent Divinity."[101] The Mediator (unknown by His name) is the one who unites by the `supreme bridge' (*pontifex maximus*) *ātman* and *brahman*.

Swami Vidyaranya in his *Panchadasi* (14 AD) deals with the indirect (*parokṣa*) and direct (*pratyakṣa*) knowledge of *Brahman*: "The knowledge that 'Brahman is' is indirect, the knowledge that 'I am Brahman' is direct." (*Panchadasi* VI, 16).[102] Panikkar writes about the direct (*pratyakṣa*) knowledge of God: "`I am *brahman*' is so far as it is not *brahman* who says so. The one who can speak thus does it only as the Spirit and the Word who is thus spoken is the Logos."[103]

F. The Son: The Mediator, `*summus pontifex*`

Panikkar, like Rahner also depends very much on the pre-Augustinian tradition, especially the thought of the Greek Fathers. Rahner argues that it is not "any one of the numerical three whom we call the persons of the one God-head [who] could become man, presupposing only that this divine person wanted to".[104] This was a trend of thought of "the theology of the schools" since the time of Augustine. "St. Augustine emphasizes that all God's activity *ad extra* is common to all three persons, since it proceeds from his one nature (*De Trinitate*, II, 17, 32) and hence, for instance, the Father could have become man if he had willed."[105] Rahner goes to the "pre-Augustinian tradition which is found especially in the Greek Fathers",[106] and says that it is precisely "the Word of God that only *he* and he alone is the one who begins and can begin a human history in case God makes the world His own ...." [107]

Panikkar affirms that only the Son, the CHRIST, can be the mediator in the Trinity:[108] "This Beginning and End of all things (Cf. Rev 1:2 etc.) has two natures, though they are not in the same mode or on the same level. It has two faces, two aspects as it were (Cf. Phil 2:7; 2 Cor 8:9; Heb 2:14). One face is turned towards the Divinity and is its full expression and its bearer (Cf. Jn 1:2; 2 Cor 4:4; Jn 6:57). The other face is turned towards the external, the world, and is the firstborn (Cf. Rom 8:29; Col 1:15,18; Rev 1:5.), the sustainer (Cf. Col 1:17; 2:10), the giver of the world's being (Cf. Col 1:16; ICor.8:6). Yet it is not two, but one--principle, one person (Cf.Jn 8:18, 21, 25, 58)."[109] Panikkar analyses this view with the insights from *Advaita*.

i. The Son is the `Thou', the Person

Even though Panikkar analyses the Trinity in the context of the *Advaita*, he maintains 'person' language in the Trinity. In the *Advaita* system particularly the attributing of person to God is not welcome. There are some Christian concepts which cause misunderstanding mainly because of the lack of correct understanding of the concepts, for instance, the concept of Persons in the Trinity.

"Hinduism is supposed neither to believe in a personal God nor to consider charity the first of religious duties. The concept of Person, which seems essential and indispensable for any exposition of Christian faith, is apparently unknown to the Hindu mind, and so on. From the other side, the more 'realized' Hindu who mostly professes *advaita* considers Christianity an inferior religion because it takes God to be essentially the 'other', allowing no union or identification with Him. For the *advaitin* the concept of person would seem secondary, and so applying it to the Absolute is tantamount to idolatry."[110]

Panikkar not only takes the *Advaita* system to give new light to the Trinity and but also attempts to prepare the *Advaita* system to accept persons in God.[111] "Personalism is not wrong in asserting that personal relationship is essential to every evolved religious attitude and that the discovery or re-velation of the God-person is a decisive contribution of Christianity."[112]

If the *mahāvākya*, "I am *Brahman*" points to the eternal I, divine transcendence, the Father, the ultimate subject of all,[113] another *mahāvākya* "*Tat tvam asi*" "that art thou" shows the second person, the "thou" in the divinity: "the thou of the I, the thou of Brahman."[114] An I is only such if there is a thou. The "thou" is totally dependent on the "I", of and from which it is the "thou" that it is.[115] The clue to the mystery of the person is the "thou". Without thou there is no "I", but only a monolithic and lifeless block in a solipsistic pit. There is only an "I" when he is capable of uttering, discovering, creating, a "thou".[116] "Because Brahman is the I, there is place for the thou: *that art thou*, thou of the I, the thou of Brahman."[117] If Father is the subject I of the "I am *Brahman*", the Son is the second person thou in "that art thou". The "thou" of the Father is the Logos, the Son whom He generated by giving Himself fully.[118] "Thou art my Son; today I have begotten thee" (Ps. 2:7). The

Son is the "thou" of the Father. The Son is the Word. "The speaker is known only in the Word."[119]

When Panikkar says that neither the Father nor the Holy Spirit are persons he does not mean to contradict the traditional understanding of the three persons in the Trinity:

Only the Son is Person, if we use the word in its eminent sense and analogically to human persons: neither the Father nor the Spirit is a Person. There is no real analogous factor (*quid analogatum*) common to the Father, the Son and the Holy Spirit. For want of a better term one could certainly call them `persons' in so far as they are real relative oppositions at the heart of the divine mystery, but one must beware of `substantialising' them or considering them `in themselves'. A person is never in himself, but by the very fact that he is a person is always a constitutive relation--*a pros ti*.[120]

Panikkar tries to be in agreement with the Hindu idea of *Brahman*, who is absolute and has no direct contact with the world. There "Brahman is not a person and consequently is not looked upon as a personal God but as the Absolute, and thus is identified with God only in the transpersonal sense expressed by the word Godhead."[121] The personal aspect cannot be attributed to *Brahman* "for if it were it would have to relate to others (things or persons), which would compromise its absoluteness. *Īśvara* is the personal aspect of Brahman, in whatever manner he may be conceived."[122] Ascribing a personal aspect to *Brahman* is equal to limiting, or reifying him.[123]*Īśvara* can be called the personal aspect of *Brahman*. The fact is that it is the problem of the relation between *Brahman* and the world that obliged Hinduism to reflect more deeply on the mystery of *Īśvara*, who is in touch with the absolute and the relative. "The concept of Brahman needs the `concrete' aspect, and this gives rise to the concept of *Īśvara* with its attendant problems."[124] It is only the Son who takes the reification, and thus only He is the Person.

ii.   **CHRIST: The Icon, Symbol of the Father**

It is to stress the visibility, the icon, the mask, the symbol of the Father that Panikkar says that only the Son is the person in the Trinity. Christ is the symbol. This symbol is not to be understood in a restricted sense. Then it will fall short of what Christian tradition understood this symbol to be.[125] The evangelical truth is that Christ is the Son, the Icon, the Image, the Word, the Glory, the Being of the Father.[126]

Brahma Sūtras states: "Origin etc., of the Universe That (is Brahman) from which (are derived) the birth etc., of this (universe)" (BS 1,1,2).[127] Panikkar distinguishes in the *Sūtra*, the 'Origin' *Brahman* and 'That from which' as the 'Origin' and the 'Relation'. According to the Brahma *Sūtra* (BS I,4,27) *Brahman* means the *yoni*, the matrix, the source:[128] "...Brahman is declared to be the source (yoni)" (BS I,4,27).[129]

There is in the Absolute Source a relation that is suggested by the expression 'from which': "That `from which' the world derives is a pure `whence', not only in relation to the World but also as such. This is to say that it is pure relation."[130] Though the Source, *Brahman*, is unoriginated, the Relation the 'from which' is originated. This can be interpreted in terms of the relation of the Father (the source, the unoriginated) and the Son (the originated, the from which). The 'that from which' "holds good in a twofold directions".[131] In St John's Prologue, there is an eternal reciprocal relation between God and Word and a relation in time with the creation: The Unoriginated God by eternally being the Father, is eternally related to the Son. The unoriginated and eternal Father, through the eternally originated Son, related in time with the cosmos by creating it. As the Son, the Logos is originated from the Father and thereupon related to the Father, the Logos is "the total manifestation of God the Father." [132] The Relation is eternal and in time, which is in the Prologue of St John that were expressed in the several confessions of faith. The Nicene Creed states: Lord Jesus Christ, the Son of God is "the only begotten born of the Father, that is of the substance of the Father, God of God, light of light, true God of true God, born, not made, of one substance with the Father..., by whom all things were made,..." (DS 54). Just as in the Nicene Creed, these relations were mentioned in several other creeds: Creed Of Epiphanius (DS 13); Nicene-Constantinopolitan Creed (DS 86); The Profession of Faith of the Council of Trent (DS 994) etc.

The image, the icon, exists: the Logos.[133] "Being is only an image, a revelation of that which, if it were completely unveiled, would not even be, for being is its manifestation, its epiphany, its symbol."[134] St Irenaeus emphasised the invisibility of the Father, but at the same time pointed out that the Son is the visibility of the Father.: "the Father is the invisible of the Son, but the Son the visible of the Father."[135]

iii. Symbol, Sacrament of the Whole Reality: CHRIST

Christ is a living symbol of the totality of reality: human, divine and cosmic.[136] He is the universal redeemer, the unifier; he unites cosmos, *anthropos* and *Theos*.[137] He is the Cosmotheandric Mystery.[138] The symbol Christ is "that symbol which `recapitulates' in itself the Real in its totality, created and uncreated." He is at the centre of the divine procession being begotten and co-inspiring. Being Alpha and Omega, He is at the centre of time. He is at "the centre of all realms of being: the divine, the angelic, the human, the corporeal the material."[139] All types of reality are represented in Him. He is the sacrament of the world and of God.[140] "Christ, the Pantocrator, is not only the universal *Redeemer* but is also--from the Father--the *creator* of everything and--along with the Spirit--is the glorifier or *divinizer* of the cosmos."[141]

iv. Christophany: Everything Exists Through CHRIST

The *Taittirīya Upaniṣad*ic "that" (TU III, 1), from which all things take their being and in which all subsist, again helps us to understand this relation of the Father, Son and the world (us). There are two orders, the natural and the supernatural having two respective movements: *ad extra* (creative) and *ab intra*, (`intratrinitarian`). Though the two orders are "different in their nature they come out of one and same ultimate act."[142] St Thomas expressed the two orders and two movements from and in God: "...God by knowing Himself, knows every creature. ...But because God by one act understands Himself and all things, His one only Word is expressive not only of the Father, but of all creatures." (ST I, q. 34, a.3.).[143]

Christ is the ontological Mediator of all that came into being. Their very existence is only because they are being mediated by Christ.[144] The Son is the Mediator, the *summus pontifex* (High Priest) of creation and also of the redemption and glorification or transformation of the world. Beings *are* in so far as they participate in the Son, are from, with and through him.[145] It is Christ, through whom all things were made and in whom all things subsist (Col. 2. 17).[146] As the very existence of every being is because of the Mediator, the whole created existence, is a Christophany. All created beings are a showing forth of Christ All created beings are a showing forth of Christ",[148] and "are on the way to becoming the one Christ",[149] the one 'Thou' of God.

Cosmos is Christophany, not only Theophany. St Paul viewed cosmos as theophany: "Ever since the creation of the world, his invisible nature, namely, his eternal power and deity, has been clearly perceived in the things that have been made." (Rom 1:20). Through 'The Five Ways' St Thomas gave proof to the existence of God through the existence of the cosmos (ST, I, q. 2, a.3)

A human person is a Christophany. A human person *is* in so far as he or she is called by the *I*. He or she is the "thou" of God only through the unique Thou, the Son called by the Father.[150]

The supreme experience is pure consciousness, but this is not self-consciousness in the sense of experience of the self. Pure consciousness is thou-consciousness where we all meet, including the I that can be experienced only as in and through the thou. There is no I-consciousness. There is only consciousness, and this is precisely the thou: the very consciousness *of* the I. The I has and is no consciousness, it is the source of it ….[151]

Philosophically one may affirm that the supreme experience, "the true and complete principle of identity, the metaphysical one and not merely logical, takes not the form of 'I am I', but the form of 'I am thou.'"[152] In the last analysis there is only a Thou of the Father, which is the Son. In God there is no multiplicity. "There cannot be two `callings' nor two `words' in God."[153] The Father calls us with the same calling with which he calls his Son.[154] We are only in so far as we participate in the Logos.

"Every being is, and is only, a *christophany*."[155] The Son, the Christ, the "Thou", through whom and for whom everything was made, is "still scattered in the many thous of the universe."[156] "`Who are you?' says…one Upanishad, speaking about ultimate liberation. `I am you', says the answer and the text continues `then he releases him' (Kaus U I,2.)." "In the non-temporal, *tempiternal*, dimension of the reality, origin, production, preservation and destruction of the world there is nothing but God, a God that, as the absolute "I", has an eternal "Thou". "This Thou, which is the Son, is the whole Christ, including the new heavens and the new earth: all beings participate in this Christ, find their place in him and are fully what they are when they become one with him, the Son."[158] It is *Īśvara* from whom they come forth, by whom they are sustained and to whom they return. "The growth of all things in time is nothing but a fuller realization of their being in *Īśvara*, says the Vedānta, and in Christ, as our *bhāsya* discloses." (Eph. 1:10; 4:2-13). [159] In the fullness of time all things will be united in Christ, "things in heaven and things on earth." (Eph. 1:10). So also, according to Panikkar, the *Brahma-Sūtra* indicated: "Whatever degree of reality this World may have, it is produced, sustained and attracted by this divine and human mediator,…" [160]

Nobody can go to God the Father (in *Advaitic* terms, nobody can become or reach and thus be the Absolute) but in and through Christ. That is to say that the mediatorship of Christ is total and unique. If something or somebody could be the link between God and the world, this would be Christ.[161] It "is what Christ stands for. If something links you to other men and to the Absolute that is Christ."[162] It is Christ "known or unknown-- who makes religion possible." Only in the Lord is there `religatio`. Christ, manifest or hidden, is the only way to God. The unique link between the created and the uncreated, the relative and the absolute, the temporal and the eternal, earth and heaven, is Christ, the only mediator. "Between these two poles everything that functions as mediator, link, `conveyor' is Christ, the sole priest of the cosmic priesthood, the Lord *par excellence*."[163]

If the Spirit causes us to cry "'*Abba*`, Father" (Gal 4:6; Rom 8:15)[164] that cry can reach the Father only through the calling of the Son to the Father.

`He who has seen me has seen the Father' is another *mahāvākya* (great utterance) of the theology of the Father. Whoever sees Christ sees the Father because the Son is the Father made visible, because there is nothing else to see of the Father except the result of his paternity, namely, the Son. But to see the Son is to see him as Son of the Father and thus to see the Father in or rather through the Son (and not in himself since he is nothing). There are not two visions or seeings, one for the Son and another for the Father: whoever sees me in the see-ing of this *me* sees the *ego* which engenders it and gives it being. Strictly speaking, one does not see *the Son* outside the Father nor the Father outside the Son. There are not two visions but one: ... 'one thing God has spoken, two things have I heard' (Ps. 61 (62) II).[165]

[1]R. Panikkar, *The Unknown Christ of Hinduism: Towards an Ecumenical Christophany*, (London: Darton, Longman & Todd; and New York: Orbis Books, 1981), p. 3

[2]Cf. Panikkar, *The Unknown...*, (1981), p. 3. Panikkar does not intend to compare God and *Brahman, Īśvara* and Christ. Cf. Panikkar, *The Unknown Christ of Hinduism*, (London: Darton, Longmn and Todd, 1964), pp. 66-67. Panikkar, *The Unknown...*, (1981), p. 99.

[3]Cf. Panikkar, "Response to H. Coward," *Cross Currents*, (Summer 1979), p. 191.

[4]Panikkar, "Response to H. Coward," *Cross Currents*, (Summer 1979), p. 191.

[5]"Dialogue in the real sense arises precisely where I (or we) discover the same currents and problems within the religion of the `other` as I (or we) find in my (or our) own religious world." Panikkar, "Silence and the Word. The Smile of the Buddha," [1969] *Myth, Faith and Hermeneutics: Cross-Cultural Studies*, (New York: The Paulist Press, 1979), p. 278.

[6]"If I have to dig out a foundation on which the other can also stand, I need his help so that he may at least be able to tell me if the ground I find is also a ground for him." R. Panikkar, "Metatheology or Diacritical Theology as Fundamental Theology" *Concilium*, (June 1969), p. 27. If Christians say that "a `Christian' truth has been discovered there. In this sense the third part of this book will discover a `Christian` truth in the Hindu tradition." Panikkar, *The Unknown...*, (1981), p. 7.

[7]Panikkar, *The Unknown...*, (1981), p. 56. Cf. Panikkar, *The Unknown...*, (1964), p. 23.

[8]St. Gregory of Nazianz [Nazianzus], *Orations*, 31, 14; as given by William A. Jurgens, *The Faith of the Early Fathers* vol. II (Minnesota: Liturgical Press, 1979), p. 33.

[9]H. Coward, "Panikkar's Approach to Interreligious Dialogue." *Cross Currents* 29 (Summer 1979), p. 184. Cf. Panikkar, *The Unknown...*, (1964), p. 10.

[10] Panikkar, The Unknown..., (1964), p. 6.

[11]Panikkar, *The Unknown...*, (1981), p. 26.

[12]Panikkar, *The Unknown...*, (1981), p. 48. cf. also Panikkar, *The Unknown...*, (1964), p. 16.

[13]Panikkar, *The Unknown...*, (1964), p. 68. Panikkar, *The Unknown...*, (1981), p. 100.

[14]Panikkar, *The Unknown...*, (1981), p. 3.

[15] Panikkar, *The Unknown...*, (1981), p. 26.

[16] Panikkar, *The Unknown...*, 1981, p. 59.

[17] Panikkar, *The Unknown...*, (1981), p. 48. If we wish union to happen within history then it is by being absorbed "into one of the

many Hindu branches." Panikkar, *The Unknown...,* (1964), p. 2.

[18] Cf. Panikkar, *The Unknown...,* (1981), p. 47.

[19] Panikkar, *The Unknown...,* (1964), p. 2.

[20]Panikkar, *The Unknown...,* (1981), p. 48.

[21]Panikkar, *The Unknown...,* (1981), p. 48.

[22]Panikkar, *The Unknown...,* (1981), p. 26.

[23] "If it is true that Śaṅkara is forced to take this viewpoint it is nonetheless true that he, according to `Scripture' (BS III, 3,39), stresses the unity of the twofold Brahman." Panikkar, *The Unknown...,* (1964), p.82. Cf. Panikkar, *The Unknown...,* (1981), p. 114.

[24]Panikkar, *The Unknown...,* (1964), pp. 66-67. Panikkar, *The Unknown...,* (1981), pp. 99, 67.

[25]Panikkar, *The Unknown...,* (1981), p. 48.

[26]Panikkar, *The Unknown...,* (1964), p. 16. "Christ is the only mediator,..." R. Panikkar, *The Intrareligious Dialogue,* (New York: The Paulist Press, 1978), p. 36.

[27]Panikkar, "Christians and so-called `non-Christians'," [1965] *Cross Currents* 22 (Summer/Fall 1972), p. 292.

[28] R. Panikkar, *The Trinity and the Religious Experience of Man:Icon-Person-Mystery,* [1970] (London: Darton, Longman and Todd, 1973), p. 45.

[29] Panikkar, *The Trinity...,* [1970] (1973), p. 46.

[30] "Advaita Vedānta, based mainly on Sahkaracārya's interpretation of the Upanisads and the Brahma Sütras, is one of the Hindu Philosophical schools that predominate in many spiritual circles today. It understands itself as the culmination of all religions and philosophies insofar as it leads to and interprets the 'ultimate experience' of nonduality, i.e., the essential non-separability of the Self (*ātman*) and 'God' (*brahman*). Among the three classical 'ways' of salvation in Hinduism, *karma* (works), *bhakti* (adoration and surrender) and *jñāna* (meditative know`ledge), this school represents the last. In fact, 'realization' or liberation' is said to be reached only by an intuitive consciousness." Panikkar, "Advaita and Bhakti. A Hindu-Christian Dialogue," *Myth, Faith and Hermeneutics...,* (1979), p. 288 n. 1.

[31] Panikkar, "Advaita and Bhakti. A Hindu-Christian Dialogue," *Myth, Faith and Hermeneutics...,* (1979), p. 288 n. 1.

[32] Panikkar, *The Trinity...,* [1970] (1973), p. 62.

[33] Alan Watts, during discussion, in Panikkar, "The Silence of the Word: Non-dualistic Polarities", [1970] *Cross Currents* (Summer/Fall 1974), p. 166.

[34]A brief description of the principal *mahāvākyāni* (the great statements) is given by John B. Chethimattam, *Indian Religions and Philosophies: Patterns of Indian Thought,* (New York: Orbis Books, 1971), pp. 56-58.

[35]Cf. Panikkar, *The Trinity...,* [1970] (1973), pp. 44-50.

[36]Panikkar, *The Trinity...,* [1970] (1973), pp. 44.

[37]*Expo. orat. domin.* PG 90, 871, as quoted by R. Panikkar, *The Trinity...,* [1970] (1973), p. 52.

[38]Panikkar, *The Trinity...,* [1970] (1973), p. 44.

[39] J. Neuner sj.. & J. Dupuis sj., ed., *The Christian Faith: in the Doctrinal Documents of the Catholic Church,* (Bangalore: Theological Publication in India, 1978), p. 103.

[40]Panikkar, *The Trinity...,* [1970] (1973), pp. 44-45.

[41] "Peter, an apostle of Jesus Christ, to the exiles...chosen and destined by God the Father and sanctified by the Spirit for obedience to Jesus Christ and for sprinkling with his blood: May grace and peace be multiplied to you. " 1 Pet 1:2.

[42]Panikkar, *The Trinity...,* [1970] (1973), p. 45.

[43]Panikkar, *The Trinity...,* [1970] (1973), p. 46.

[44]Panikkar, *The Trinity...,* [1970] (1973), p. 46.

[45] (DS 805) Neuner & Dupuis, *The Christian Faith...,* (1978), p. 105, (ND 319).

[46]Panikkar, *The Trinity...,* [1970] (1973), p. 46, cf. pp. 9-69; cf. also R. Panikkar, "Towards an Ecumenical Theandric Spirituality," *Journal of Ecumenical Studies,* 5 (1968), pp. 507-534. E. Cousins, "Raimundo Panikkar and the Christian systematic theology of the Future," *Cross Currents,* 29 (Summer 1979) p. 147. "It is the immolation or the mystery of the Cross in the Trinity." Panikkar, *The Trinity...,* [1970] (1973), p. 60.

[47]Panikkar, *The Trinity...*, [1970] (1973), p. 68.

[48]Panikkar, *The Trinity...*, [1970] (1973), p. 48.

[49]Panikkar, *The Trinity...*, [1970] (1973), p. 46.

[50] Clement of Alexandria *The Stromata* (or *Carpets*) 5, 12, 82 *Ante-Nicene Fathers.*, as cited by Johannes Quasten, *Patrology* Vo. II: *The Ante-Nicene Literature After Irenaeus,* (Westminster: Christian Classics, Inc., (1950) 1984, p. 22.

[51]Clement of Alexandria *The Stromata* (or *Carpets*) 5, 12, 82 *Ante-Nicene Fathers.*, as cited by Johannes Quasten, *Patrology* Vo. II: *The Ante-Nicene Literature After Irenaeus,* (Westminster: Christian Classics, Inc., (1950) 1984, p. 22.

[52]Panikkar, *The Trinity...*, [1970] (1973), pp. 46-47.

[53]Panikkar, *The Trinity...*, [1970] (1973), p. 47.

[54]Panikkar, *The Trinity...*, [1970] (1973), p. 78.

[55] Ignatius of Antioch, *Letter to the Magnesians*, 8,2; as quoted by William A. Jurgens, *The Faith of the Early Fathers* vol.I (Minnesota: Liturgical Press, 1970), p. 19.

[56] Ignatius of Antioch, *Letter to the Romans*, 8,2; as quoted by William A. Jurgens, *The Faith of the Early Fathers* vol.I (Minnesota: Liturgical Press, 1970), p. 22. ".... The virginity of Mary, her giving birth, and also the death of the Lord, were hidden from the prince of this world:- three mysteries loudly proclaimed, but wrought in the silence of God." *Letter to the Ephesians*, 19, 1; as quoted by William A. Jurgens, *The Faith of the Early Fathers* vol.I (Minnesota: Liturgical Press, 1970), p. 18.

[57]Panikkar, *The Trinity...*, [1970] (1973), p. 47. Cf. also, Panikkar, "Silence and the Word...," [1969] in *Myth, Faith and Hermeneutics,* (1979), p. 268, cf. p. 273.

[58] "God is that about which there can be no talk. Discourse on God is basically inauthentic; only in the interior cell where the *logos* is silent can the Father be adored in spirit and truth." Panikkar, "Silence and the Word...," [1969] in *Myth, Faith and Hermeneutics,* (1979), p. 268, cf. p. 273.

[59]Panikkar, *The Trinity...*, [1970] (1973), p. 47.

[60]Panikkar, *The Trinity...*, [1970] (1973), pp. 47-48.

[61]Cf. Robert Ernst Hume, *The Thirteen Principal Upanishads* (Translated from the Sanskrit), (New Delhi: Oxford University Press, (1921) 1984), p. 372. Cf. Panikkar, *The Unknown...*, (1981), p. 135. Panikkar, *The Unknown...*, (1964), p. 105.

[62]Panikkar, *The Unknown...*, (1981), p. 97.

[63]Panikkar, *The Unknown...*, (1964), pp. 79-80. Panikkar, *The Unknown...*, (1981), pp. 112, 108.

[64]Panikkar, *The Trinity...*, [1970] (1973), p. 48. Modern atheists or nihilists "are not outside the *oikumene*, these atheists who reject the god-idol so often worshipped by the religions of the world. Rather are they the present-day witnesses to a spirituality which was directed to the Father but to a Father `severed' from the living Trinity. They are bearing witness to the truth that no one can ever see the Father, because, in the final analysis, there is *nothing* to see." Panikkar, *The Trinity...*, [1970] (1973), p. 78.

[65]Panikkar, *The Trinity...*, [1970] (1973), p. 48.

[66]Panikkar, *The Trinity...*, [1970] (1973), p. 47. The case is similar with *Brahman:* "Now because the question of Being always starts from an analysis of beings, and beings in their mobility point towards their own non-existence, Brahman had also to encompass non-Being (CU VI, 2,1; TU II,7.)." Panikkar, *The Unknown...*, (1981), p. 135. Panikkar, *The Unknown...*, (1964), p. 105-106.

[67]Panikkar, *The Trinity...*, [1970] (1973), p. 49.

[68]Cf. Panikkar, *The Trinity...*, [1970] (1973), p. 68.

[69]Panikkar, *The Trinity...*, [1970] (1973), p. 47.

[70]Cf. Panikkar, *The Trinity...*, (1975), pp. 44-50, 58.

[71]Cf. Panikkar, *The Trinity...*, (1975), pp. 63-64, 58.

[72]Panikkar, *The Trinity...*, [1970] (1973), pp. 58-59. Cf. also Panikkar, "...Theandric Spirituality," *Journal of Ecumenical Studies,* 5 (1968), pp. 507-534. Cousins, "...Theology of the Future," *Cross Currents,* 29 (Summer 1979), pp. 147-148.

[73]Panikkar, *The Trinity...*, [1970] (1973), p. 46.

[74]Panikkar, *The Trinity...*, [1970] (1973), pp. 49-50.

[75]Panikkar, *The Trinity...*, [1970] (1973), p. 62, cf. p. 61.

[76] Mühlen, Heribert. Der Heilige Geist als Person (Münster: Münsterliche Beitrag zur Theologie, 1967), pp. 1-4, 11-16.

[77] Panikkar, "Silence and the Word...," [1969] *Myth, Faith and Hermeneutics*, (1979). p. 287.

[78] Panikkar, "Silence and the Word...," [1969] *Myth, Faith and Hermeneutics*, (1979). p. 287.

[79]The Eleventh Council of Toledo on divinity (ND 308, DS 525), Cf. Neuner & Dupuis, *The Christian Faith...*, (1978), p. 99.

[80]The Eleventh Council of Toledo on divinity (ND 309, DS 526) Cf. Neuner & Dupuis, *The Christian Faith...*, (1978), p. 99.

[81]Panikkar, *The Trinity...*, [1970] (1973), p. 63. Cf. R. Panikkar, *The Vedic Experience. Mantraman~jarī: An Anthology of the Vedas for Modern Man and Contemporary Celebration*, [1977] (London: Darton, Longman and Todd, 1979), p. 702.

[82]Panikkar, *The Trinity...*, [1970] (1973), p. 68.

[83]Panikkar, *The Trinity...*, [1970] (1973), p. 63.

[84]Panikkar, *The Trinity...*, [1970] (1973), p. 63. Cf. Panikkar, *The Vedic Experience...*, [1977] (1979), p. 702.

[85] "*Ātman* is *brahman*, but it is not said that *brahman* is *ātman*, if we allow the verbal form *is* (*bhavati*) to carry the dynamism of the process of identification." Panikkar, *The Vedic Experience...*, [1977] (1979), p. 702. "`S is P' does not imply that P (qua S) is S (qua P), but only that P (qua P) is S (qua S); so that `S is P' but not vice versa without Subject and Predicate becoming meaningless." Panikkar, *The Vedic Experience...*, [1977] (1979), p. 702 n. 68.

[86]Panikkar, *The Vedic Experience...*, [1977] (1979), p. 703.

[87] "For example, when we say `John is good' or `water is liquid,' or `God is,' or `five is more than three,' in each instance the verbal form is depends on the subject and the predicate it unites, for each time it expresses a different relation....John is not good in the same sense that five is more than three. John can cease to be good...John's is depends on his very being." But five would cease to be five if it is cease to be more than three. "...the five's is depends on the nature of the five." Panikkar, The Vedic Experience..., [1977] (1979), p. 703

[88]Panikkar, *The Vedic Experience...*, [1977] (1979), p. 703.

[89]Panikkar, *The Vedic Experience...*, [1977] (1979), pp. 703-704.

[90]Panikkar, *The Vedic Experience...*, [1977] (1979), p. 702.

[91] Panikkar, The Vedic Experience..., [1977] (1979), p. 705.

[92] Kaushitaki Brahmana Upanishad, Translated by Dr. A. G. Krishna Warrier, Published by The Theosophical Publishing House, Chennai, Published | Modified on July 27th, 2019. https://www.shastras.com/upanishads-rig-veda/kaushitaki-brahmana-upanishad/ Cf. also Panikkar, *The Vedic Experience...*, [1977] (1979), p. 702as quoted by Panikkar, *The Vedic Experience...*, [1977] (1979), p. 710.

[93] Panikkar, The Vedic Experience..., [1977] (1979), p. 702

[94] Panikkar, *The Vedic Experience...*, [1977] (1979), p. 710.

[95]Panikkar, *The Trinity...*, [1970] (1973), p. 64. Cf. Panikkar, *The Vedic Experience...*, [1977] (1979), p. 702-703.

[96] Panikkar, "Silence and the Word...," [1969] *Myth, Faith and Hermeneutics...*, (1979), pp. 287-288. Cf also Panikkar, *The Vedic Experience....*, [1977] (1979), pp. 747-753.

[97] Panikkar, "Silence and the Word...," [1969] *Myth, Faith and Hermeneutics...*, (1979), pp. 287-288. Cf also Panikkar, *The Vedic Experience....*, [1977] (1979), pp. 747-753.

[98]Panikkar, *The Trinity...*, [1970] (1973), p. 64.

[99]Panikkar, *The Trinity...*, [1970] (1973), pp. 64-65.

[100]Panikkar, *The Trinity...*, [1970] (1973), p. 63.

[101]Panikkar, *The Trinity...*, [1970] (1973), p. 64. The recognition of "the *ātman-brahman* equation amounts to the discovery of the overall span under which the whole of reality is inscribed. It means realizing that transcendence has no real meaning except in relation to immanence, that the ultimate reality of everything is not different from ultimate reality as such, precisely because the arch *ātman-brahman* overspans the whole of reality and expresses its unity." Panikkar, *The Vedic Experience...*, [1977] (1979), p. 703.

[102]Sri Vidyāraṇya Swāmi, Pancadasi, (14 A.D), *English Translation and Notes*, By Swāmi Swāhānanda, Mylapore, Madras: Sri Ramakrishna Math, 1967, p. 131, cf also Panikkar, *The Trinity...*, [1970] (1973), p. 64. Panikkar, *The Vedic Experience...*, [1977] (1979), p.

76.

[103]Panikkar, *The Trinity...*, [1970] (1973), p. 64.

[104] K. Rahner, "Jesus Christ," in *Foundations of Christian Faith: An Introduction to the idea of Christianity.* Translated by William V. Dych. (New York: Crossroad, 1984), p. 214.

[105] K. Rahner, "Trinity in Theology," in *Encyclopedia of Theology: A Concise Sacramentum Mundi,* edt. by Karl Rahner, (London: Burns & Oates, 1981), p. 1762.

[106] K. Rahner, "Jesus Christ," in *Foundations of Christian Faith: An Introduction to the idea of Christianity.* Translated by William V. Dych. (New York: Crossroad, 1984), p. 214.

[107] K. Rahner, "Jesus Christ," in *Foundations of Christian Faith: An Introduction to the idea of Christianity.* Translated by William V. Dych. (New York: Crossroad, 1984), p. 214.

[108]Panikkar, *The Trinity...*, [1970] (1973), p. 53.

[109] Panikkar, *The Unknown...*, (1981), p.156-157. Panikkar, *The Unknown...*, (1964), pp. 126-127.

[110] Panikkar, "Advaita and Bhakti. A Hindu-Christian Dialogue," *Myth, Faith and Hermeneutics...*, (1979), p. 278.

[111] Cf. Panikkar, "Silence and the Word...," [1969] *Myth, Faith and Hermeneutics...*, (1979), pp. 278-288.

[112] Panikkar, *The Trinity...*, (1975), p. 54.

[113]Cf. Panikkar, *The Vedic Experience...*, [1977] (1979), pp. 727-729.

[114]Panikkar, *The Vedic Experience...*, [1977] (1979), p. 749.

[115]Panikkar, *The Vedic Experience...*, [1977] (1979), p. 747.

[116]Panikkar, *The Vedic Experience...*, [1977] (1979), p. 748.

[117]Panikkar, *The Vedic Experience...*, [1977] (1979), p. 749.

[118]Panikkar, *The Trinity...*, (1975), p. 46.

[119]Panikkar, *The Trinity...*, (1975), p. 61.

[120]Panikkar, *The Trinity...*, [1970] (1973), p. 52.

[121]Panikkar, *The Unknown...*, (1981), p. 134. Cf. Panikkar, *The Unknown...*, (1964), pp. 104-105.

[122]Panikkar, *The Unknown...*, (1981), p. 152. Panikkar, *The Unknown...*, (1964), p. 122.

[123]Cf. J. Dupuis, sj., "Trinity and World Religions." *Clergy Monthly*, 35 (Feb. 1971), pp. 79-80.

[124]Panikkar, *The Unknown...*, (1981), p. 143. Panikkar, *The Unknown...*, (1964), p. 114.

[125]Panikkar, *The Unknown...*, (1981), p. 29.

[126]Panikkar, *The Trinity...*, (1975), p. 55. .

[127]*Brahma Sutra*, Translated by Swami Gambhirananda, Published by Advaita Ashram, Kolkatta, June 18th, 2019, Vedanta Spiritual Library | www.celextel.org , also in Panikkar Panikkar, *The Unknown...*, (1981), p.155. Panikkar, *The Unknown...*, (1964), p. 126.

[128] Panikkar, *The Unknown...*, (1981), p. 157 n., 143.

[129]*Brahma Sutra*, Translated by Swami Gambhirananda, Published by Advaita Ashram, Kolkatta, June 18th, 2019, Vedanta Spiritual Library | www.celextel.org

[130] Panikkar, *The Unknown...*, (1981), p. 157. Cf. Panikkar, *The Unknown...*, (1964), pp. 127.

[131] Panikkar, *The Unknown...*, (1964), pp. 127. Cf. Panikkar, *The Unknown...*, (1981), p. 157.

[132] Panikkar, *The Unknown...*, (1981), p. 157; Cf. Panikkar, *The Unknown...*, (1964), pp. 127.

[133]Panikkar, *The Trinity...*, [1970] (1973), pp. 48-49.

[134]Panikkar, *The Trinity...*, [1970] (1973), p. 49.

[135]St. Irenaeus, *Against Heresies* Book IV, Chapter 6, 6. https://www.newadvent.org/fathers/0103406.htm , cf. also Panikkar, *The Trinity...*, [1970] (1973), p. 49.

[136]Panikkar, *The Unknown...*, (1981), p. 27.

[137]"Any Christ who is less than a Cosmic, Human and Divine Manifestation will not do." Panikkar, *The Unknown...*, (1981), p. 26.

[138]Cf. Panikkar, "Colligite Fragmenta: For an Integration of Reality." in F.A. Eigo, S.E. Fittipaldi eds., *From Alienation to At-Oneness. Proceedings of the Theology Institute of Villanova University*. (Villanova: The Villanova University Press, 1977), p. 74.

This *mysterium conjuctionis* is CHRIST the meeting point, mid-point, the centre of the whole cosmotheandric mystery. Cf. E. Cousins, "Raimundo Panikkar and the Christian systematic

Theology of the Future," *Cross Currents*, 29 (Summer 1979), p. 149.

[139]Panikkar, *The Unknown...*, (1981), p. 28.

[140]Panikkar, *The Unknown...*, (1981), p. 28.

[141]Panikkar, "...`non-Christians‘," [1965] *Cross Currents*, 22 (1972), p. 293.

[142] Panikkar, *The Unknown...*, (1981), pp. 157-158. Cf. Panikkar, *The Unknown...*, (1964), pp. 127-128.

[143] Cf. Panikkar, *The Unknown...*, (1981), p. 158 n. 144.

[144]"Christus ist der ontologische Mittler; des Seienden -- die `gemachten' Dinge also -- sind eben deswegen Sein, weil sie an Christus teilhaben." Panikkar, "Extra Ecclesiam nulla salus. Die innere Unzulänglichkeit einer nicht- christischen Welt", *Neues Abendland*, X, (May 1955), p. 261.

[145]R. Panikkar, *The Trinity...*, p. 54.

[146]Panikkar, "...`non-Christians‘," [1965] *Cross Currents*, 22 (1972), p. 285.

[147]Cf. Panikkar, *The Trinity...*, p. 54; Panikkar, "...`non-Christians‘," [1965] *Cross Currents*, 22 (1972), p. 285; R. Panikkar, "Dialogue between Ian and Ray: Is Jesus Christ unique?" Raimundo Panikkar and Ian Stephens, *Theoria to Theory*, Vol. I (Jan. 1967), p. 131.

[148]R. Panikkar, *The Trinity...*, p. 54.

[149]Panikkar, "...Christ unique?" *Theoria to Theory*, (1967), p. 131.

[150]Panikkar, *The Trinity...*, [1970] (1973), p. 68.

[151]Panikkar, "The Supreme Experience: The Ways of East and West," [1970] *Myth, Faith and Hermeneutics...*, (1979), p. 308.

[152]Panikkar, "The Supreme Experience:..," [1970] *Myth, Faith and Hermeneutics...*, (1979), p. 308.

[153]Panikkar, *The Trinity...*, [1970] (1973), p. 68.

[154]Panikkar, *The Trinity...*, (1975), p. 68.

[155]Panikkar, *The Trinity...*, [1970] (1973), p. 68.

[156]Panikkar, *The Trinity...*, [1970] (1973), p. 69.

[157]Panikkar, "The Supreme Experience:..," [1970] *Myth, Faith and Hermeneutics...*, (1979), p. 308.

[158]Panikkar, *The Unknown...*, (1981), p. 161. Cf. Panikkar, *The Unknown...*, (1964), pp. 130-131.

[159]Panikkar, *The Unknown...*, (1981), p. 162. Cf. Panikkar, *The Unknown...*, (1964), pp. 130-131.

[160]Panikkar, *The Unknown...*, (1981), p. 162. Cf. Panikkar, *The Unknown...*, (1964), p. 131.

[161]Panikkar, "...`non-Christians'," *Cross Currents* 22 (1972), p. 295.

[162]Panikkar, "...Christ unique?" *Theoria to Theory*, (1967), p. 131.

[163]Panikkar, *The Trinity...*, (1975), p. 53. "Whatever happens to be the door is door because Christ is there." Panikkar, "...Christ unique?" *Theoria to Theory*, (1967), p. 132.

[164]Panikkar, *The Trinity...*, [1970] (1973), p. 68.

[165]Panikkar, *The Trinity...*, [1970] (1973), p. 49.

TWO

2 Religions Meet in the Mediating Mystery, Christ

Religions can meet in the Universal and the Only Mediating Mystery, the CHRIST. As every being *qua* being is a Christophany, there is no real relation outside or independent of Christ; there is no communication without Christ. There is no human relation from which Christ is absent. Wherever there are two or more gathered in His name, there He is present (Mt 18:20).[1] Only the CHRIST, who began the ontological mediatory function from the beginning of creation, can cause the mediation between religions. "Only in Christ are the meeting and the embrace possible."[2]

CHRIST, the meeting point, signifies the whole mystery of the Mediator, the centre of reality.[3] It is the ultimate mystery,[4] or rather, we can say, it is "the ultimate mediating mystery". Though mediating and liberating it is an ever hidden mystery which transcends all names.[5] Coward clarifies the meaning of Panikkar's unifying CHRIST: The principle of Panikkar is Christ is the criterion for all inter religious encounter. It is "founded on the epistemological claim that the Christian revelation contains the truth of reality to a degree which transcends all other religions."[6]

The goal is interfaith encounter through dialogue, understanding and finally the conversion and the unity of all religions to the essence of the Christian revelation, the Christ logos", the "one stripped of sectarian religious forms, "the mystical Christ logos."[7] Panikkar states that the encounter of religions is not in the Greek name of CHRIST, but in the cosmotheandric principle; a christocentric theology, even without the Greek name of Christ being mentioned. CHRIST "does not stand only for one single event but for that cosmotheandric principle which, being incarnated in Jesus of Nazareth, has not only spoken many times through the prophets (Cf. Heb 1:1) but also has not left himself without witness in any moment of history (Cf. Acts 14:17)."[8] The Christian symbol for this reality is CHRIST, and the historical manifestation of this reality is Jesus.[9] The latter is not the meeting point. "Christ the Lord and Saviour is for the Christian, the symbol of that mystery which is unveiled in or through Jesus."[10] The meeting point is CHRIST, and possibly Hinduism and Christianity can meet in that common ground which is CHRIST. Even the adjective `Christian` must not be viewed in a restrictive sense; "it indicates anything endowed with the richness of that reality for which Christians have no other name than Christ."[11]

A. Christianity and Hinduism Meet in CHRIST

In speaking of the reality "which Christians call Christ", Panikkar is trying to achieve a meeting of the two religions. Panikkar is trying to achieve a meeting of the two religions. "For, it is impossible to declare something common and a meeting point if it is already possessed and monopolized by only one party. It must be common to both. In fact, Christianity has no exclusive claim over CHRIST, "Christ does not belong to Christianity; he belongs to his Father only."[13] Panikkar may be reminding us of the words of Paul: "For all things are yours,...whether...the world or life or death or the present or the future, all are yours; and you are Christ's; and Christ is God's" (I Cor. 3: 21b-23). Instead of Christianity possessing Christ, Christ possesses both Christianity and Hinduism. "It is Christianity and Hinduism as well, that belong to Christ, though in two different levels."[14]

The "theandric reality which Christians call Christ"[15] is common. Christianity and Hinduism both express and unfold their belief in the theandric mystery, though in two different ways.[16] The epistemological claim of Panikkar is that "Christian revelation contains the truth of reality to a degree which transcends all other religions." This is in accord with his principle that Christ is the criterion for all inter-religious encounter which has to take place in history.[17] Therefore, "Christianity and Hinduism both meet in Christ. Christ is their meeting-point. The real encounter can only take place in Christ, because only in Christ do they meet."[18] In 1981, Panikkar clarified this meeting point. The common encountering point is "in a reality which partakes of both the Divine and the Human ...." This reality "Christians cannot but call Christ."[19] Hinduism and Christianity can meet in the divine-human reality that Christians call Christ.

B. Presence of Christ in Hinduism

CHRIST is not the God of a particular religion. He is not a God among other gods, nor is He to displace other gods. He is not one of the avatars. On the other hand, He is the Lord of creation and of history. He is the Lord of the gods. He is the hidden one under the faces of all real and honest beloved gods. In those gods the face of the Lord is hidden, waiting for a full revelation. It is He who receives the prayers of the peoples, when they sincerely and lovingly worship their gods. He is the unknown receiver of all good works.[20] CHRIST is "efficient and present in any authentic religion, regardless of its name and form."[21] In fact, the aim of one of the important works of Panikkar is to show: "that there is a living Presence of Christ in Hinduism."[22] It is the Christian expectation that "Christ comes at the end of time and that all religions may be pointing towards Him, who shall be the expectation of the peoples (Rom 15:12; etc.)."[23] But "Christ is not only at the end but also at the beginning."[24] This will help us to realize that "Christ is the beginning and end of all religion."[25] "Christ is not only the ontological goal of Hinduism but also its true inspirer, and His grace is the leading, though hidden, force pushing it towards its full disclosure (Jn 1:1; 9-10)."[26]

If religions are relating human beings with the Absolute CHRIST, the *religatio* is already there.[27] In other religions He may not be recognized as Jesus[28] or as Christ.[29] Yet the real and not only the nominal link to the transcendent,[30] that which holds everything and which makes us more than our present selves, that in which everyone, in one or other form, believes that mediator, or the way, or whatever name we may give to it,[31] is, by the above definition, the Christ.[32] He relates everybody. His attitude and function "is one of inclusivity, and not of exclusivity."[33] He excludes no religion. Christ is the way whether one is aware of it or not. "In the Gospels people are told they did things to Christ when they didn't know it (Mt 25:40)."[34] He is present and effective, though in a more or less hidden and unknown way, in every human being and religion.[35]

C. Presence of CHRIST in Hindu Sacraments

CHRIST was present in Hinduism not only when *ṛṣis* composed the Hindu sacred scriptures but also now. He is active in Hinduism and in the Hindu sacraments. One can conclude this from the Christian conviction: "Christ is the universal redeemer. There is no redemption apart from him."[36] White light appears as different colours in the context of a prism. In the context of human nature, the only ultimate Saviour, CHRIST who enlightens and saves all men and women, is experienced differently, giving rise to different religions.[37]

God leads humankind to their fulness, to Himself.[38] God provides every human person coming into existence with the means for salvation.[39] The human person has to find these means provided by God in the positive and concrete religions of humankind.[40] It is God who hears prayers of the peoples. It is through their concrete religions that they strive towards God; and, in fact, it is God Himself who gives impetus to all their religious strivings. Thus, the Son of God, CHRIST, the only mediator between humankind and God, really stands behind all true forms of worship and religious life. It is He who accepts and hears the prayers of all people of all religions. It is He who reminds them that they belong to one family and have a supernatural destination of sharing in the life of God Himself. It is He who gives them the grace and the power to discover the true face of God.[41]

God is the only author of salvation and CHRIST as God is the only saviour. The Hindu is saved in the total religious context provided by that religion. Though it may be true to say that the Hindu is saved not on account of Hinduism, he or she is not saved in spite of it, but in and through it. "If Christ is the one Saviour of all men it may be said that Christ is in Hinduism too, though unknown and unrecognized."[42] Hinduism "is a kind of Christianity in potency, because it has already a Christian seed, because it is the desire of fullness, and that fullness in Christ, is already pointing towards it, already contains, indeed, the symbolism of the Christian reality"[43].

The fact that, like Judaism, Hinduism does not accept Christianity, does not in any way mean that CHRIST is not there already present.[44]

D. Footprints of the Saviour in Other Religions

It is not very difficult to find the footprints of the saviour in other religions when one analyses the historical, anthropological/ sociological and theological aspects of religions.

i. **History of Religions: Gospel Values in the Religions**

From an empirical and ontological study of the history of religions it is evident that some of the Gospel values (for example universal love and love for our enemies, returning a blessing for a curse and recognizing everywhere human--superhuman--dignity) were found in many other religions even centuries before Christ.[45]

An ontological study of history from a theological point of view proves again that divine providence has been looking after all his children, and that there is a Christian economy in history...in which it (Hinduism) would find its providential place. What other means of salvation has God-Christ provided to the people of India down the ages, even before the appearance of historical Christianity, if not Hinduism?[46]

In the ultimate sense salvation takes place in the unutterable depths of the human person. For this the more tangible channels of the established religions have a prominent role to play, "even if they cannot provide the perfect means of salvation."[47]

i. **God Through Socio-Religious Structures**

Anthropological and social considerations show that the reciprocal relation of God and the human beings is, not purely individualistic, but also through the community, through the social and religious structures.

We cannot simply be satisfied with the explanation that people of other religions are saved by their individual conscience. This individualistic, characteristically European, approach is unthinkable for the Indian people. "Man in Hinduism is still immersed in a collective consciousness, he still has cosmic instincts which lead him through life with more certainty than the security that a `modern' man may have in his own `private' reason."[48] According to Panikkar everyone is bound by history, geography and race. One cannot simply be an individual. One is a father, mother, brother, sister, son etc., and member of a particular nation, society, firm etc., at the same time. Religion is not concerned with the abstract human person or his or her pure nature. It wants to be the way or the good news for the concrete and historical human nature. It speaks a certain language, takes on a particular character, puts on the particular garb which the necessity of space, time, race and culture demands. The human person is situated in a particular social structure. His or her religion also must suit the sociological structure and must not be a pure abstraction. God must speak in a language that is somehow available to people. God's message also must be presented in a particular form, concept, or picture with a particular message. In short, the outer form of a religion also belongs to the nature of that religion.[49] So a particular religion, even though different from Christianity, can contain the way towards salvation.

iii. Theological: Christ the Primordial Sacrament in the Religions

The means of salvation that God provides for the Hindus are not totally separate from their religion. God deals with creation and with humankind not in a disorderly manner, but in a "natural and supernatural pattern which crystallises in what we call the physical and the historical order."[50] That salvation, which is a supernatural act--"for it is the union with God, or the full incorporation into Christ, in Christian terms"--[51] also has a normal and ordinary means by which God /CHRIST leads peoples and individuals to Himself. The normal and ordinary means of salvation are sacraments in the Church.[52] Ultimately these sacraments are signs and symbols of the primordial sacrament, CHRIST himself (cf. Eph., 1: 4-9; 3: 3-6; Col. 1: 26; 2: 2). If we consider the concept of sacrament, not in the restricted sense of the Tridentine sacraments of the New Law,[53] but in the general sense of scholastic philosophy, one can speak also of the sacraments of the Old Testament and of the *sacramenta naturae* (sacraments of nature),[54] "then we may well say that sacraments are the ordinary means by which God leads the peoples of the earth towards Himself."[55] The efficacy of the Christian sacrament is not magical. The efficacy depends on the action of Christ within those instruments of grace.[56] We may assume that other sacraments cannot have the same efficacy.[57] "Christian doctrine emphasizes the distinction between the sacraments of the new Covenant and all other *sacraments* (Cf. D 845; 857) and points out that those of the Old Law did not cause grace [were only a figure of grace] (Cf. D 695) but just symbolised it: ...."[58] However, Christ may be active and effective in the human being that receives either class of sacraments.[59] "A good and *bona fide* Hindu is saved by Christ ...,through the sacraments of Hinduism, through the *Mysterion* that comes down to him through Hinduism ...."[60] By sacraments of Hinduism Panikkar does "not mean exclusively the Hindu *Saṃskāras* which have been losing momentum in modern Hinduism, but also other means, signs and symbols provided by Hinduism."[61] Every religion which deserves this name represents a more or less perfect way towards God, a covenant with the divine, in whose midst, Christ works and accomplishes his merciful work.[62]

The sacraments in religions are "sacraments in the cosmic covenant" or "cosmic sacraments".[63] Every religion shows (reveals) a covenant, a cosmic covenant that God had made with Adam, Noah and so on. This does not in any way reduce the uniqueness of God's covenant with Abraham.[64] The relation between the Old Covenant and the New Covenant is clear. Now the Church has to take into account the history of humankind before the Old Covenant to find out the relation between the Cosmic Covenant and the New Covenant.[65] The mission of the Church is not one of segregating other religions and declaring them to be heathen as the rulers of Israel once did, but that of loving and uniting. This dimension is in the economy of the New Covenant. In the canon of the sacrifice of Christ, in the Mass, there are remembrances of the offerings of Abel, Melchisedek and Abraham.[66] This is according to the mind of Christ. When Christ showed that He had a real grasp of the Old Testament He meant He had a deep knowledge of the Cosmic testament, of which a portion is included in Hinduism.[67]

[1]Panikkar, "...'non-Christians'," *Cross Currents* 22 (1972), p. 292.

[2]Panikkar, *The Unknown...*, (1964), p. 25.

[3]"In this book Christ stands for that centre of reality, that crystallization-point around which the human, the divine and the material can grow." Panikkar, *The Unknown...*, (1981), p. 27. Rama, Krishna, *Īśvara*, Purusha may be other such names. Panikkar, *The Unknown...*, (1981), p. 27.

[4]Panikkar, *The Unknown...*, (1981), p. 49 n., 13.

[5]Panikkar, *Salvation in Christ: Concreteness and Universality; The Supername*, (Santa Barbara, 1972), p. 16.

[6] Coward, "Panikkar's...Dialogue," *Cross Currents*, (Summer 1979), p. 186.

[7] Coward, "Panikkar's...Dialogue," *Cross Currents*, (Summer 1979), p. 186. Coward depends ofn on Panikkar's *The Trinity and the Religious Experience of Man* (Mayknoll, N.Y. 1975), pp. 3-4, 54; *The Unknown Christ of Hinduism*, (London, 1964), p. xi, 6; "Inter-Religious Dialogue: Some Priciples", *Journal of Ecumenical Studies* 12 (Summer 1975) p. 409.

[8] Panikkar, *Salvation in Christ:..*, (1972), p. 72.

[9] Panikkar, *The Unknown...*, (1981), p. 5. Panikkar, *Salvation in Christ:..*, (1972), p. 59.

[10] Panikkar, *Salvation in Christ:..*, (1972), p. 59.

[11] Panikkar, *The Unknown...*, (1981), p. 5.

[12]Panikkar, *The Unknown...*, (1981), p. 37. The "reality...what Christians cannot but call Christ" p. 37. Cf. also Panikkar, *Salvation in Christ:..*, (1972), p. 79.

[13]Panikkar, *The Unknown...*, (1981), p. 54.

[14]Panikkar, *The Unknown...*, (1964), pp. 20-21. "...the Christ who confronts Hinduism is the same who confronts Christianity. *There are not two Christs....*" Panikkar, "Confrontation between Hinduism and Christ", *Logos*, 10 (1969), p. 51.

[15]Panikkar, *The Unknown...*, (1981), p. 37.

[16]Panikkar, *The Unknown...*, (1981), p. 54.

[17]"This is a claim which Panikkar seems to make not only as a believer, but also as a scholar of comparative religion." Coward, "Panikkar's...Dialogue," *Cross Currents*, (Summer 1979), p. 186. Cf. Panikkar, *The Trinity...*, (1975), pp. 3-4, 54; cf. Panikkar, *The Unknown...*, (1964), p. xi, 6; cf. Panikkar, "Inter-Religious Dialogue...", *Journal of Ecumenical Studies* 12 (Summer 1975) p. 409.

[18]Panikkar, *The Unknown...*, (1964), p. 6. "Christ is the common meeting ground, the point of encounter in all inter-religious dialogue." Coward, "Panikkar's...Dialogue," *Cross Currents*, (Summer 1979), pp. 184-185. Cf. Panikkar, *The Unknown...*, (1964), p. 5.

[19]Panikkar, *The Unknown...*, (1981), p. 37.

[20]"Er ist der Herr der Schöpfung und der Geschichte, der Herr der Götter, das verborgene und doch zu offenbarende Antlitz aller echt und aufrichtig angebeteten Götter, der unsichtbare

Empfangende einer jeden guten Tat." Panikkar, *Die vielen Götter und der eine Herr: Beiträge zum Ökumenischen Gespräch der Weltreligionen,* (Weilheim/Oberbayern: Otto Wilhelm Barth, 1963), p. 16.

[21]Panikkar, "Inter-Religious Dialogue...", *Journal of Ecumenical Studies* 12 (Summer 1975) p. 409. "Christ is present and effective in any authentic religion, whatever the form or the name." Panikkar, *Intrareligious Dialogue,* (1978), p. 36.

[22]Panikkar, *The Unknown...,* (1964), p. ix. Cf. Coward, "Panikkar's...Dialogue," *Cross Currents,* (Summer 1979), p. 185.

[23]Panikkar, *The Unknown...,* (1964), pp. ix-x.

[24]Panikkar, *The Unknown...,* (1964), pp. x.

[25]Coward, "Panikkar's...Dialogue," *Cross Currents,* (Summer 1979) p. 185.

[26]Panikkar, *The Unknown...,* (1964), p. x.

[27] Panikkar, *The Trinity...,* (1975), p. 53. Panikkar, "...`non-Christians`," [1965] *Cross Currents,* 22 (1972), p. 282.

[28] Panikkar, "...Christ unique?" *Theoria to Theory,* (1967), p. 131.

[29] In non Christian religions "Christ is not explicitly acknowledged as the Lord." Panikkar, "...`non-Christians`," *Cross Currents* 22 (1972), p. 282.

[30] Panikkar, "...Christ unique?" *Theoria to Theory,* (1967), p. 131.

[31] Panikkar, "...Christ unique?" *Theoria to Theory,* (1967), p. 131.

[32] Panikkar, "...Christ unique?" *Theoria to Theory,* (1967), p. 131.

[33] Panikkar, "...Christ unique?" *Theoria to Theory,* (1967), p. 131.

[34] Panikkar, "...Christ unique?" *Theoria to Theory,* (1967), p. 132.

[35] Panikkar, "...Christ unique?" *Theoria to Theory,* (1967), p. 131.

[36]Panikkar, *The Unknown...,* (1964), p. 33.

[37]"Nach dem Christentum würde dieses weiße Licht der lebendige Christus sein, der jeden Menschen erleuchtet, der in diese Welt kommt. Die verschiedenen Farben kommen nur zustande, wenn dieses weiße Licht auf das Prisma der menschlichen Natur fällt und verschiedene Wellenlängen annimmt." Panikkar, *Religionen und die Religion* (München: Max Hüber, 1965), p. 151.

[38]Panikkar, *Religionen...,* (1965), p. 15.

[39]Panikkar, *The Unknown...,* (1964), p. 51.

[40]Cf. Panikkar, *Die vielen Götter...*, (1963), p. 121.

[41]Panikkar, *Religionen...*, (1965), p. 15.

[42]J.B.Chethimattam, cmi., "Indian Approaches to Christology: R. Panikker's approach to Christology." *The Indian Journal of Theology* 23 (1974), pp. 219-220.

[43]Panikkar, *The Unknown...*, (1964), pp. 59-60.

[44]"Die Tatsache, daß der Hinduismus das Christentum nicht anerkennt, so wie sich das Judentum gegen seine christliche Erfüllung wehrt, bedeutet keinesweges, daß Christus dort nicht schon gegenwärtig, noch daß der Ausdruck 'Hindu-Katholizisums' sinnlos ist." Panikkar, *Die vielen Götter...*, (1963), p. 133.

[45]Cf. Panikkar, "Christians and so-called `non-Christians`." in *Christian Revelation and World Religions* (London: Burns and Oates, 1967), edt., J. Neuner sj. (London 1967) pp. 145ff. Cf. also Panikkar, *The Unknown...*, (1964), pp. 48-49.

[46]Panikkar, *The Unknown...*, (1964), p. 49.

[47]Panikkar, *The Unknown...*, (1964), p. 50. Cf. also W. Bierbaum, "Geschichte als Paidagogia Theou,--Die Heilsgeschichtslehre des Klemens von Alexandrien," *Münchener Theologische Zeitschrift* V, 4, Munich, 1954, pp. 246-272.

[48]Panikkar, *The Unknown...*, (1964), p. 55.

[49]Cf. Panikkar, *Religionen...*, (1965), pp. 83-84.

[50]Panikkar, *The Unknown...*, (1964), pp. 51-52.

[51]Panikkar, *The Unknown...*, (1964), p. 52.

[52]Panikkar, *The Unknown...*, (1964), p. 53.

[53]Cf. Conc. Trident. Sess. VII, *De Sacramentis*, D 844, sq.

[54]Cf. Thomas Aquinas, ST I-II, 9 [*sic* q.] 102, a. 5; and III, q. 60 and 61. [art.3; cf. also q. 62 art.6]., as given by Panikkar, *The Unknown...*, (1964), p. 53.

[55]Panikkar, *The Unknown...*, (1964), p. 53. `R.d.q. sacramenta sunt necessaria ad humanam salutem--' Thomas Aquinas, ST III, 9. [*sic* q.] 61, a. 1, and also *ante Christum*, ibid., a. 3., as given by Panikkar.

[56]"The sacraments when presented scientifically can appear as mechanical instruments of grace (*ex opere operato*) instead of the personal acts of Christ using this means to unite mankind with the

Father by the loving power of the Holy Spirit. (The term *ex opere operato*, properly understood, means *ex opere operantis Christi*.)" E. Zeitler, `Our Liturgical Programme' in *The Clergy Monthly*, XXIII, 5 (July 1959), p. 175, as quoted by Panikkar, *The Unknown...*, (1964), p. 53.

[57]Panikkar, *The Unknown...*, (1964), pp. 53-54.

[58]Panikkar, *The Unknown...*, (1964), p. 54 n.1.

[59]Panikkar, *The Unknown...*, (1964), p. 54.

[60]Panikkar, *The Unknown...*, (1964), p. 54.

[61]Panikkar, *The Unknown...*, (1964), p. 54 n. 5.

[62]"Jede Religion, die diesen Namen verdient, stellt einen mehr oder weniger vollkommenen Weg zu Gott, ein Bündnis mit dem Göttlichen dar, in dessen Mitte Christus wirkt und Seine Gnadentat vollbringt." Panikkar, *Die vielen Götter...*, (1963), p. 121.

[63]Panikkar, "...Christians and ...non Christian..," in *Christian Revelation...*, edt. J. Neuner sj., (London 1967), 50.

[64]Panikkar, *Die vielen Götter...*, (1963), p. 121; cf. p. 124.

[65]"...es (ist) die Befugnis der ganzen Kirche.., die Verbindung zwischen dem Neuen Bund und diesem anderen kosmischen `Gesetz' zu finden." Panikkar, *Die vielen Götter...*, (1963), p. 122.

[66]"Man ist nicht zufällig im 'Kanon'des Opfers Christi bei der Messe des Abel, Melchisedek und Abraham eingedenk."Panikkar, *Die vielen Götter...*, (1963), p. 124.

[67]Christus kann zu einem Juden sagen, "daß er ein tieferes und wahreres Verständnis seiner heiligen Bücher besitze, auch den tiefen und wahren Sinn des Kosmischen Testamentes, von dem ein Teil im Hinduismus enthalten ist...." Panikkar, *Die vielen Götter...*, (1963), p. 132.

THREE

3 CHRIST: THE UNKNOWN MEDIATOR

The CHRIST present in Hinduism and its sacraments is the Unknown Christ. It is not *"The Hidden Christ*, as though Christians knew the secret and Hindus did not."[1] The Unknown Christ is neither one who is unknown to Hindus and known to Christians nor vice versa. The `unknown‘ Christ of Hinduism can be either unknown, or known *qua* Christ, to Christians and Hindus alike.[2] There is a reality which is unknown, *qua* Christ, to both Christians and Hindus.[3] The followers of both the religions cannot consider themselves "as possessors of truth, but as beings possessed by a truth that is greater than we are and which cannot be known because knowing is possessive, is of the self which must end in order to accept the new life."[4] It is the mystery hidden for long ages in God.[5] He is, for the moment, veiled.[6] The real face, image, icon of the living God and the saving truth is hidden or distorted by a veil.[7] The unknown or hidden aspect shows the superior nature of the mystery. It is this mystery CHRIST that is present in Hinduism. The `Unknown Christ of Hinduism' remains unknown "and yet continues to be Christ."[8] CHRIST, even though unknown, is not a stranger to Hinduism. He is the real light that illumines everyone in the world: "...that unknown reality, which Christians call Christ, discovered in the heart of Hinduism, not as a stranger to it, but as its very principle of life, as the light which illumines every Man who comes into the World (Cf. Jn 1:9)." [9]

A. Christ, Unknown in Christian Mysticism.

The mysterious, unknown aspect of Christ is not totally unknown to the mystical understanding of Christian tradition: the Unknown Christ of Hinduism, i.e. the mysteric aspect "is also present in Hinduism, according to the mystical understanding of Christian Tradition. Directly they come to the belief that Hinduism is recognized as a true religion, Christians will find themselves obliged to call this mysteric aspect 'Christ'."[10] He is the expectation of the peoples (Gen 49:10), His spirit is at work among non-believers (Rom 15:21 quoting Isa 52:15). He is already found by those who do not seek Him (Rom 10:20; cf. Isa 65:1). He is the hidden God of Isaiah 45:15; and the unknown God of Acts 17:23. He is the one present in the hearts of the people of good will (Cf. Luke 2:14).[11] Just as the kingdom of God is not visibly noticeable, so too, after the resurrection, Christ himself is not always recognizable (Lk 24:13-16ff; Jn 20: 14.).[12] Christ's thirty years of hidden life continues down through the centuries.[13] And it will always continue, for "...Christ will never be totally known on earth, because that would amount to seeing the Father whom nobody can see."[14]

A. **Not Bringing *in*, but Unveiling Christ in Hinduism**

In order to have an *ecumenical ecumenism[15]* the Christian is also obliged to recognize and name this hidden mystery, `CHRIST`, instead of bringing "*his* conception of Christ to the other peoples and religions ...." the Christian is also obliged to recognize and name this hidden mystery, `CHRIST`, instead of bringing \"his conception of Christ to the other peoples and religions....\""[17] "The Christian attitude is not ultimately one of bringing Christ *in*, but of bringing Him *forth*, of discovering Christ".[18] It means the un-veiling of reality.[19] This bringing Him forth will help towards the full growth of Christ in Hinduism; it will help to really continue the Incarnation of the Son of God; it will also help towards revealing His true name, His actual deeds, His wondrous message.[20] One can observe that "this re-vealing does not mean that full Christianity is already there".[21] Where Christ is not explicitly acknowledged as the Lord,[22] 'the unveiled truth' will have to receive the re-vealed fulness of Christ.[23]

C. The Unknown God of Athenians[24], CHRIST of Hinduism

The fulness of Christ can be realized both by Christianity and by Hinduism only at the end.[25] Yet Panikkar wants the unity between Hinduism and Christianity to be achieved in history. Even though Christians have not yet fully known Christ, they consciously confess Christ as Lord. In this particular context, Christianity has something special to do. Christianity has to preach the Christ, 'the unknown Christ'. It has to detect the footprints of the unknown Christ not only in Christianity but also in Hinduism and show or reveal it to the Hindus. If the Christian faith is to truly represent the fullness that comes at the end of time, then its function is not only to enrich another religion or advocate one spirituality against another. There must be a revelation, that is, an unveiling of the mystery that is hidden just there, in the world religions. The essence of the Christian kerygma is not so much that it is a proclamation, but that it announces a proclaimer.[26]

St Paul preached to the Greeks in the Areopagus: "What...you worship as unknown, this I proclaim to you" (Acts 17: 23). This was not just a stratagem on St Paul's part. Rather, he was unveiling "a true face of God, he did not proclaim *another* God".[27]

St Paul inspires us to speak not only of "the unknown God of the Greeks, but also of the *hidden Christ of Hinduism*-- hidden and unknown and yet present and at work because he is not far from any one of us." St Paul had to prevent the Christ mystery from falling either into the Judaizing tendency to make Christianity into a reformed sect of Judaism (Romans and Galatians) or into the Greek mentality which inclined to absorb Christianity into a kind of gnosis or a variety of Greek wisdom (Cf. 1 and 2 Cor). "In both cases the struggle was the same--against the attempt to minimize the figure of Christ and interpret it apart from the central mystery of the Trinity."[28] St Paul struggled to show "how in Christ the mystery of God has been revealed, and how he the Pantocrator, the cosmic redeemer, the beginning and end of all things, the only begotten, the Logos is at the same time Jesus, son of Mary, crucified by men and risen from the dead so that he may sum up the whole of creation in himself and lead it back to God the Father, gathering together all the scattered pieces (Cf. Jn 6:12) of wandering humanity, of a Mankind which remains full of expectancy, because the children of God are still to be made known (Cf. Rom 8:19)."[29]

The situation of living in the midst of the Hindu religion is not very different from that of Paul passing through the city of idols. When we carefully study Hinduism and its sacred scriptures, we will find occasions for seeing the unknown Christ. Panikkar gives plenty of Hindu Scriptural, particularly Upanisadic, citations[30] to show not the doctrinal parallelism[31] but perhaps a symbolic or functional parallelism. Some of the functions or qualities of Christ as the mediator are narrated in the Hindu Scriptures.

There comes to our attention the great cosmological hymn of the *Ṛg-Veda*: "What God shall we adore with our oblation?" ("*kasmai devāya haviṣā vidhema*") (RV 10, 121, 1-9).[32] "`To the Unknown God,` *Deo ignoto*, is the title that, since the days of Max Müller, has usually been given to this solemn hymn of praise and glorification of the Supreme ...."[33] The question in the rigvedic verse is not, in fact, a question, it discloses the name of God. This name is not a proper name but it is the interrogative pronoun, simply *ka* (who?) or, more exactly, *kasmai* (to whom?). This is "the name of *Prajāpathi*, the Father of all beings."[34] The question *kasmai* (to whom?) is repeated in verses 1-9. In verse 10 comes as an answer in vocative '*Prajāpathi!*' (*prajāpate*).[35] Thus the text shows "the mysterious character of the Godhead, which can never be fully grasped and hence is only fittingly approached by an open interrogation. What at the Areopagus was a dedication in the dative is here a question in the dative: God is the `to whom?' of our search."[36] The name of God is an interrogative pronoun because, "God is not a substance and has no name, but he is a question, a simple question, a simple pronoun, an interrogative pronoun."[37] From the awareness that the name of God is simply an interrogative, one finds that this interrogative name is a question about God. "To find him means to seek him; to know him means not to know him (to name him means to invoke him as an unknown God with an unknown name), for his name is the question, pure and simple."[38] There takes place a kind of Pauline proclamation of Christ by seeing the unknown God in Hinduism, for "...recognizing the presence of *God* in other religions is equivalent to proclaiming the presence of Christ in them, `for in him all things subsist' (Col 1:17)."[39] "God is at work in all religions: the Christian kerygma does not proclaim a new God, but the mirabilia of God, of which the Mystery of Christ hidden in God is the alpha and omega (Cf. Eph 3:9; Rom 16:25, etc.)".[40] The Christ who comes face to face with Hinduism, "is a Christ who was in the beginning before Abraham, who is the Creator, Alpha and Omega, the only Son and also the first-born of all creatures.[41] Panikkar discovers in the heart of Hinduism, "that unknown *reality*, which Christians call Christ...not as a stranger to it, but as its very *principle of life* ...."[42]

D. *Sahasra nāma* of the Unknown Christ

In Hinduism there is no altar dedicated to an unknown god. All temples and altars are dedicated to particular deities. People are worshipping the unknown Christ, but under other names. Christians must reveal the unknown Christ under the names of those deities. When Hindus are chanting *sahasra nāma*, the thousand names, in fact they are invoking the unknown Christ, the Word, who "did have and is having the `ten thousand' echoes of a polyphonic symphony."[43] The appearance may be Krishna, but the reality is CHRIST. The rope and snake analogy of Indian philosophy is extremely helpful here. What the Christian has to do is to reveal the real state of affairs: there is no snake but only a rope. The appearance may sometimes be that of *Krishna*, or of society, or of man, or of an idol, but in reality, it is a rope, "a simple rope and indeed a rope of salvation."[44] The case is somewhat similar to Mary Magdalene's misunderstanding and anxiety about the resurrected Christ; and Christ removed her doubt. If the bronze serpent of Moses[45] gave salvation in the desert, for The Wisdom of Solomon this bronze snake was "*symbolon sōtērias*, `symbol of salvation'" (Wis 16:6f);[46] and Christ saw it as a symbol of Himself (Jn 3:14). Will Christ find the symbols of the Hindu religion symbolizing Himself? The different symbols proper to the particular traditions express the same religious truth that belongs to and is recognised by both.[47] By interpreting God and the world according to *Brahma-sutra* 1,1,2. Panikkar shows:

the presence of religious truth within more than one religion, and how unveiling of that truth may be to the mutual enlightenment of all concerned. Now, when a religious truth is recognized by both parties and thus belongs to both traditions, it will be called in each case by the vocabulary proper to the particular tradition recognizing it. If Christians, believing in the truth of their own religion, recognize truth outside it, they will be inclined to say that a `Christian' truth has been discovered there. In this sense the third part of this book will discover a `Christian' truth in the Hindu tradition.[48]

i. **Mediator Christ in Other Names**

Christ is the only Mediator who is present also in other religions in which the binding together of God and the world takes place. "The Western Christian tradition with its theistically charged language has identified it with the historical Jesus, whereas some of the fundamental Hindu intuitions concerning this Centre refer to Brahman, Atman, *vāc*, *bindu* and other symbols of the Absolute according to different contexts."[49] The main tenor of Panikkar is that the mediating principle will be called by a variety of names: "Christ presents the fundamental characteristics of the mediator between divine and cosmic, eternal and temporal, etc., which other religions call *Īśvara, Tathāgata* or even Jahweh, Allah and so on--at least when they are not seeking to distinguish between a *saguna*and *nirguna*Brahman."[50] "We could equally well call him, say, *Īśvara*, or by any other name pointing towards the same function...."[51] Consequently, Hindus can both experience and articulate this presence of CHRIST. It is this "Christ that other religious traditions call by a variety of names."[52] The Hindus may not find much difficulty in subscribing to the Chalcedonian confession concerning Christ.[53] Together with the Council of Chalcedon, 451 (DS 148) the Christians believe that God and Christ are indivisible, inseparable, at the same time without mixture and fusion. That means God is at work in the world, as it were, is always in and through Christ.[54] But Hindus will call Christ the Mediator as *Īśvara* or *Bhagavan*.[55] "...the Christ the Christian comes to proclaim is Christ present, active, unknown, and hidden within Hinduism .... This Christ present, active, unknown and hidden may be called Isvara, Bhagavan, or even '*Krsna*', `*Narayana*` or `*Siva*'."[56]

ii. 'Messiah' in Judaeo-Christian, not in Hindu Religious Context

Thrusting the Christian names of CHRIST on the Hindu religious context is of no avail.[57] For example, we cannot simply transplant Peter's confession "Thou art the Messiah, the Son of the living God" (Mt 16:16), into the Hindu religious context. Messiah makes no sense to them. Outside Peter's Jewish context, where there is no expectation of a messiah, the Petrine confession may not be intelligible.[58] If the Petrine affirmation Mt 16:16 is translated literally "into any of the Indian languages, including the classical, it is bound to convey almost the opposite meaning of what a Christian would think he says. To affirm in fact that Jesus is the Messiah is to confirm India in her suspicion that Jesus has nothing to do with her, with her traditions and longings; to underscore that he is the Son of God, even in a peculiar way, is for India almost a truism and only the beginning of any spiritual message worth the name."[59] As far as the Son of God is concerned, the Hindu will reply: Well, we are all sons of God.[60]

iii. **The Mission: Revealing the Unknown Presence of CHRIST**

Some of the biblical assertions have relevance in the context of the Judaeo-Christian world, but, in the context of the world religions, they are extrapolations. "No law in physics or mathematics is valid outside the interval for which it is formulated and beyond which one must be careful not to extrapolate unduly."[61] This is also relevant to some extent to the Biblical world view. The sayings in the Jewish or middle-eastern context must not be projected onto other cultural contexts.[62] The text "Thou art the Messiah, the Son of the Living God." (Mt 16:16) is unintelligible outside the Judaeo-Christian context. The Messiah is He who has been desired, hoped for, awaited. But Hinduism has never awaited anyone and has never shared Israel's hope. It means nothing to her to be told that Christ is the Messiah. Perhaps Hindus will accommodate Him but not as a universal saviour.[63]

What is important for us is to reveal the unknown Christ -- the Alpha and Omega, the Only Son and also the First-born of all creatures, who thus can transcend all names -- who comes face to face with Hinduism.[64] We have to present CHRIST taking into account the context instead of simply repeating the traditional terms which have relevance in the Judaeo-Christian context. In the new context there may be fitting terms that signify the reality of the Mediator and which will enable people to know the real sense of the Mediator. St Paul in his epistle to the Romans (10:20) tries to present Christ in the non-Jewish context by quoting Isaiah: "I have been found by those who did not ask for me" (Is 65:1). Here the accent is not on the Messiah.[65]

iv. **The Nomenclature CHRIST[66]**

Panikkar finds the common meeting point between Christianity and Hinduism. But in naming this meeting point he does not accept a strategic neutral position--for example, he does not give it a secular name. His is not a diplomatic approach either--he does not call it by a name more acceptable to Hinduism. He goes on calling the meeting point Christ. The simple reason is that Christ is the name Christians use to express the reality which mediates between the world and God. At "first sight it really looks ridiculous if not preposterous from a Hindu point of view to say that the encounter takes place in Christ." There is a need to clarify the issue as it stands. The initial reason for choosing the term, Christ, is that there is no "corresponding Hindu symbol" At \"first sight it really looks ridiculous if not preposterous from a Hindu point of view to say that the encounter takes place in Christ.\" There is a need to clarify the issue as it stands.[68] The initial reason for choosing the term, Christ, is that there is no \"corresponding Hindu symbol\" "to express the unity between the Absolute and the relative.[69] In Hinduism not only is there a plurality of symbols, "but no symbol as a rule contains the pluralistic polyvalence as does the symbol of Christ."[70] Perhaps the name Rāma, which is totally human and totally divine, may serve: "...Rāma is material and spiritual, temporal and eternal." Here again all Hindus may not agree.[71] Consequently: "The statement ... Christ as the place of encounter makes sense, at least for the Christian, and can be made understandable--if not acceptable--to the Hindu also, if an equivalent (homoeomorphic) statement is made about Śiva, Krisna or Kālī."[72] When one searches for the meeting-point between two religions, and has found it in the mystery common to both the religions it is natural to call that mystery with the terminology available in one's own religion.[73] Panikkar, as a Christian, chooses the term Christ. He could have used more general terms such as Lord,[74] Being, Logos,[75] yet he prefers[76] the term Christ. This is not due to any apologetic[77] intention but because of the term's own intrinsic depth of meaning. Even though it is so often "microdoxically" viewed, experienced, and believed in[78]--so that the selection of this name may appear sectarian,[79]--in the light of historico-sociological considerations we can affirm that Christ is still for one quarter of humanity a living symbol.[80] Towards this, "one of the most powerful symbols of humankind",[81] we must not entertain the attitudes of fanaticism or agnostic relativism[82] or iconoclasm.[83] There is need for a constructive approach. A deepening and even conversion may be more constructive than mere destruction. The true encounter of religious traditions is, like the religious quest itself, arrived at by deepening the very sense of our belief,[84] by "deepening and enlarging that particular symbol [Christ] and no other."[85] The motive force for such an approach is a philosophical one. We need today an encounter in the "depth of ultimate symbols." The presupposition "is that the power of the symbol may be so enlarged and deepened that each symbol--even if it is primarily and directly meaningful in that environment in which it originated--opens up experiences and realities not (yet) intended in the actual symbol."[86] Thus the `Christ-symbol', 'the living symbol', will assume a universal aspect, and be valid not only for Christians or for sectarian religiosity.[87] By appropriate interpretation or experience, "Christ can be one of the living symbols capable of giving a center...to the rich variety and depth of human experience."[88] The final result is religious. The name Christ will appropriately serve for the ideal unity of religions. By enlarging and deepening the Christian understanding of the mystery of Christ,[89] "the symbol Christ" would become "an appropriate `partner'...for the mutual enriching of the human experience as it reaches toward harmony, a deeper consciousness and realization of oneness, without monochromatic uniformity." When we come to the fulness of meaning of the figure of Christ,[90] this name, more than other names, effectively connotes the connection between the absolute and the relative.[91] "That theandric `thing', the concrete connection between the Absolute and relative which all religions recognize in one way or another" may be called `Christ'. For, "the Christian concept, though of Hebrew origin and connected with the Judaic tradition, has precisely this function."[92] Thus this name will serve as an appropriate "symbol of the cosmotheandric unity."[93]

v) Universality of the Symbol, 'Christ'

The Christian symbol should not be sectarian, it should have a universal significance.

Any symbol, today, which is meaningful only for a group of men is bound to become sectarian, unfit for worship, specially for Christian worship, which due to its very nature possesses a claim to universality. The saving action of Christ in which Christians believe and for which they have the support of Scripture and Tradition is truly universal or, to put it in the words of a council, `as there never has been, is or shall be a man whose nature was not assumed in Christ, so there never was, shall be or is a man for whom Christ did not die' (D 319). A symbol which excludes anybody or makes any type of discrimination can today hardly be called a Christian symbol, or a symbol fit for Christian worship.[94]

Thus, when Christianity says that salvation is universal (not restricted to a particular religion), and that salvation is only through Jesus Christ--the Lord of History--it means Christianity presents this Christian symbol as universal. This symbol for universal salvation cannot be objectified, reified or restricted to "a mere historical personage."[95] As a result, the redemptive work of the *messiah* reaches the whole of humankind: "Christ died and rose again for all men--before and after him--his redemption is universal and unique."[96] Further, the universality of the redeemer cannot be confined within the boundaries of humankind. Christ assumes cosmic dimensions: In Christ everything was summed up (Eph. 1:10); and consequently, "he is the atonement not only for our sins, but for the defilement of the whole world" (cf. I Jn 2:2).[97]

E. **Meet in the Differently Known One Lord**

Even though the Unknown Christ can be known differently, intentionally and analogically all meet in the common ground, the One Lord.[98]

i. The Intentional Level: (Existential Realm)

By the intentional level, Panikkar means the underlying existent reality that a concept intentionally means, that which lays bare the intentionality of the concept. When two people of different religious traditions pray, their prayer is leading to something. Ultimately, that something is intentionally the same, that is, the divine reality.[99] The future Catholic encounter with Hinduism should be informed by this `ontic-intentionality'.[100]

ii. The Analogical Level: (Essential Realm)

Christians call Christ the Lord just as Hindus call *Īśvara* the Lord. The meaning they give to the word Lord, however great the difference may be, cannot be so absolute as to transcend all analogy. The word Lord is an analogous one and has several meanings, which are, however, not totally different. "What is the *primum analogatum*, the primordial principle that enables us to call the Lord not only by separate names, but also to refer to him by two different concepts?"[101]

a. Interpreting Differently, Pointing to the One Mystery

Every religion has three aspects: i. The socio-historical structure, z; ii. The sacramental structure and symbols, y;[102] and iii. the mystery, x. The third level has a dimension of transcendence, of freedom and initiative, which Christians along with others call the divine. This is totally outside human manipulation. Here the Christian worships the mystery but has no criteria to say that it is not the same mystery behind and beyond every longing of the human heart and grasping of the human mind. "The transcendental convergence here may be much greater' so that people belonging to different religions z and having conflicting interpretations of *y* may still be pointing towards the same *x*. And my contention is that Christ is one of the names of this mystery."[103] In any human tradition these threefold levels exist.[104] There is a distinction between these three levels (not separation). Any believer lives in *z* by means of *y* pointing towards *x*. Red *z* is not violet *x*, and yet "there is no solution of continuity between the colors of the spectrum. Where red *z* ends and orange *y* begins is very often a question of sensitivity."[105] These three levels are necessary: "indeed, my experience of the Mystery is not independent of my vision of the sacramental structure, and this latter is subsidiary to my insertion in a socio-historical milieu. We cannot go directly to *x*; we cannot even point towards it outside our *y*, and independently of our *z*."[106] "Now, affirming that Christ is one of the symbols for *x*, I am not degrading other symbols. I am only emphasizing that we meet in the center ...."[107]

b. **Religious Symbols Functionally Equal to Jesus Christ**

The Mediator, a cosmotheandric mystery, participates in the whole reality. "Any Christ who is less than a Cosmic, Human and Divine Manifestation will not do."[108] Conversely every "being is a *Christophany*, a showing forth of Christ."[109] If every being can show forth CHRIST and can function as a symbol of CHRIST, a religious symbol can more intensely symbolize CHRIST. And thus, the religious symbols can be functionally equal to Jesus Christ, the Christian symbol of CHRIST. Phenomenologically, Christ presents the fundamental characteristics of the mediator between divine and cosmic, eternal and temporal, etc., which other religions call *Īśvara,Tathāgata* or even Jahweh, Allah and so on....It is not without a deep and prophetic intuition that much of neo-Hindu spirituality speaks in this way of `christic awareness'."[110] That is why it often happens that when a Christian describes Christ to a Hindu, the Hindu thinks that the Christian is talking about Krisna.[111]

[1]Panikkar, *The Unknown...*, (1981), p.26.

[2]Panikkar, *The Unknown...*, (1981), p. 26.

[3]To this unknown x "the name `Christ' could be applied once it is made clear that both sides can make a meaningful use of it." Panikkar, *The Unknown...*, (1981), p. 26.

[4] Panikkar, *The Unknown...*, (1981), p. 50.

[5]Panikkar, *The Unknown...*, (1964), p.25. In Panikkar, *The Unknown...*, (1981), p.59.

[6]Panikkar, *The Unknown...*, (1964), p.25.In Panikkar, *The Unknown...*, (1981), p. 59.

[7]Cf. Panikkar, "...`non-Christians'," [1965] *Cross Currents*, 22 (1972), p. 297.

[8]Panikkar, *The Unknown...*, (1981), p. 30. "...any religion is mysteriously orientated towards Christ and Christ, mysteriously but no less really, works within it." Panikkar, "Church and the World Religions," [1966] *Religion and Society*, XIV, (No. 2, 1967), p. 63.

[9]Panikkar, *The Unknown...*, (1981), p. 20.

[10]Panikkar, *The Unknown...*, (1981), p. 26.

[11]Panikkar, *The Unknown...*, (1981), p. 88.

[12]Panikkar, *The Unknown...*, (1981), p. 13.

[13]"...not only is God a 'hidden God' (Is 45:15), but also that Christ is having a follow-up of twenty centuries of his thirty years of occult life" (Cf. Jn 7:3-5; Col 3:3; etc.) Panikkar, *The Unknown...*, (1964), p.xiii.

[14]Panikkar, *The Unknown...*, (1981), p. 8.

[15]ecumenical ecumenism, cf. Menacherry, Cheriyan. *Confluence of Religions, Panikkar's Christological prayāṇa 1*, Chisinau, Moldova: Blessed Hope Publishing, 2022, pp. 34-35.

[16]Cf. Panikkar, *The Unknown...*, (1964), p. 31; Panikkar, *The Unknown...*, (1981), pp. 65-66.

[17]Panikkar, *The Unknown...*, (1981), p. 30.

[18]Panikkar, *The Unknown...*, (1964), p. 45.

[19]Panikkar, *The Unknown...*, (1964), p. 45.

[20]Panikkar, "...`non-Christians'," [1965] *Cross Currents*, 22 (1972), p. 297.

[21]Panikkar, *The Unknown...*, (1964), p. 45.

[22]Panikkar, "...`non-Christians'," [1965] *Cross Currents*, 22 (1972), p. 282.

[23]Panikkar, *The Unknown...*, (1964), p. xi.

[24] The Unknown God or Agnostos Theos (Ancient Greek: Ἄγνωστος Θεός) "was not so much a specific deity, but a placeholder, for whatever god or gods actually existed but whose name and nature were not revealed to the Athenians or the Hellenized world at large." https://www.hellenicaworld.com/Greece/Mythology/en/UnknownGod.html

[25]The expression Christ is the *alpha* and *omega* in fact declares "that Christ is not yet 'finished', not 'discovered‘, until the 'last moment‘ or 'end‘ has come. The process itself is still open-ended." Panikkar, *The Unknown...*, (1981), p. 168.

[26]"Soll der christliche Glaube die Fülle, die am Ende der Zeiten kommt, wirklich darstellen, so kann er nicht nur eine Religion befruchten und viel weniger eine Spiritualität gegen eine andere befürworten, sondern er muß eine Offenbarung, d.h. eine Entschleierung des Mysteriums sein, das gerade dort, in den Weltreligionen verborgen ist....Das Wesen des christlichen Kerygmas besteht nicht so sehr darin, daß es eine *Verkündigung* ist, sondern daß es einen *Verkündiger* kund gibt." Panikkar, *Kerygma und Indien. Zur heilsgeschichtlichen Problematik der christlichen begegnung mit Indien*, (Hamburg: Herbert Reich, 1967), pp. 9-10.

[27]Panikkar, *The Unknown...*, (1981), p. 168. Panikkar, *The Unknown...*, (1964), p. 137.

[28]Panikkar, *The Unknown...*, (1981), pp. 168-169. Panikkar, *The Unknown...*, (1964), pp. 137-138.

[29]Panikkar, *The Unknown...*, (1981), pp. 168-169. Panikkar, *The Unknown...*, (1964), pp. 137-138.

[30]Cf. Panikkar, *The Unknown...*, (1981), p. 49 nn., 13, 14, 15, 16 and 17: Cf. Panikkar, *The Unknown...*, (1981), p. 49 n., 13, 14, 15, 16 and 17.

Cf. TU II 9,1). Cf. SU II,4; III,3; III,9; III,11; III,16 etc. BU 1,4,7; II,4,5; TU II.6,1 CU III, 14,2. Cf. KathU II,2 3; MundU III.2.3: SU I.6; II,4; III,4; III,8; III,20; CU III,15,3; BG 1X,2 3; X,10-11; XVIII,56: 58; 62. Cf. MundU II,2,2ff., SU III,12: CU III,14,1. Cf. KathU V,15; MundU II. 2.9-10. etc.; SU

III,12; 17, etc., CU III,12,8-9; III,13,7; III,17,7-8.

[31]These "references illustrate something more than merely doctrinal parallelisms, since both traditions put these texts in the context of the quest for the ultimate mystery...." Panikkar, *The Unknown...,* (1981), p. 49 n., 13.

[32] RV.X, 121. 1-9, The question is repeated in RV. X.121 verses 1c, 2c,3c, 4c, 5c, 6c, 7c, 8c, 9c. Translated by Ralph T. H. Griffith, https://www.sacred-texts.com/hin/rigveda/rv10121.htm

Transliteration, http://www.sanskritweb.net/rigveda/rigveda.pdf

Cf. Panikkar, *The Vedic Experience...,* [1977] (1979), pp. 67-72.

[33]Panikkar, *The Vedic Experience...,* [1977] (1979), p. 67.

[34]Panikkar, *The Vedic Experience...,* [1977] (1979), p. 69.

[35] Translated by Ralph T. H. Griffith, https://www.sacred-texts.com/hin/rigveda/rv10121.htm

Transliteration, http://www.sanskritweb.net/rigveda/rigveda.pdf

[36]Panikkar, *The Unknown...,* (1981), p. 168.

[37]Panikkar, "Silence and the Word...," [1969] *Myth, Faith and Hermeneutics...,* (1979), p. 267.

[38]Panikkar, "Silence and the Word...," [1969] *Myth, Faith and Hermeneutics...,* (1979), p. 267.

[39]Panikkar, *The Unknown...,* (1981), p. 169. Instead of "the presence of Christ" in 1961 the expression was the action of Christ in those fields." Panikkar, *The Unknown...,* (1964), p. 138.

[40] Panikkar, *The Unknown...,* (1981), p. 168. Panikkar, *The Unknown...,* (1964), p. 137.

[41]Panikkar, "...Hinduism and Christ", *Logos,* 1969, p. 50.

[42]Panikkar, *The Unknown...,* (1981), p. 20.

[43] "Our concern has been to unearth a little that underlying myth which peoples of the world are beginning, that the Word that was at the beginning, did have and is having the `ten thousand' echos of a polyphony symphony." Panikkar, *Salvation in Christ:...,* (1972), p. 81.

[44]Panikkar, "...`non-Christians'," [1965] *Cross Currents*, 22 (1972), p. 297.

[45] Panikkar alludes to Moses rising the bronze serpent Num. 21. 6-9; Jn 3. 14. Cf. Panikkar, "...`non-Christians'," *Cross Currents* 22 (1972), p. 306, n. 40.

[46]Bruce Vawter, cm., "The Gospel According to John," in *Jerom Biblical Commantary*, edts, Brown, R. E., J. A. Fitzmyer and R. E. Murphy, (London: Geoffrey Chapman, 1984), 63:70.

[47]Panikkar, *The Unknown...*, (1981), p. 7. There is "the presence of the one Mystery...in both traditions." Panikkar, *The Unknown...*, (1981), p. 26.

[48] Panikkar, *The Unknown...*, (1981), p. 7. There is "the presence of the one Mystery...in both traditions." Panikkar, *The Unknown...*, (1981), p. 26.

[49] Panikkar, *The Unknown...*, (1981), p. 51. [not in Panikkar, *The Unknown...*, (1964), p.19.

[50] Panikkar, *The Trinity...*, (1975), p. 54.

[51]Panikkar, "...Christ unique?" *Theoria to Theory*, (1967), p. 133.

[52]Panikkar, *The Trinity...*, (1975), p. 54.

[53] Panikkar, The Unknown..., (1964), pp. 23 24.

[54] Panikkar, The Unknown..., (1964), pp. 23 24.

[55] Panikkar, *The Unknown...*, (1964), pp. 23-24. Compare: "Hindus would...perhaps call it *Īśvara* (Lord) or *Bhagavān*." Panikkar, *The Unknown...*, (1981), p. 56.

[56]Panikkar, "...Hinduism and Christ", *Logos*, 1969, p. 51.

[57]Panikkar, *The Unknown...*, (1981), p. 51. (not in Panikkar, *The Unknown...*, (1964), p. 19).

[58] Cf. Panikkar, *Salvation in Christ:...*, (1972), pp.23-24

[59] Panikkar, "The Relation of the Gospels to Hindu Culture Religion." in Donald G. Miller and D.Y. Hadidian, eds., *Jesus and Man's Hope*, vol. II., (Pittsburgh: Theological Seminary, 1971), p. 252. Cf. Panikkar, "...Hinduism and Christ", *Logos*, 1969, p. 50. Cf. Panikkar, *Salvation in Christ:...*, (1972), pp.23-24.

[60]Cf. Panikkar, "...Hinduism and Christ", *Logos*, 1969, p. 50. "It is more than I could believe that Jesus was the only incarnate son of

God, and that only he who believed in him would have everlasting life. If God could have sons, all of us were His sons. If Jesus was like God, or God Himself, then, all men were like God and could be God Himself." M.K.Gandhi, *An Autobiography of the Story of my Experiments with Truth,* Boston (Beacon Press), 1957, p. 136; as quoted by Panikkar *Salvation in Christ:..,* (1972), p. 24, n.2.

[61]Panikkar, "...Hinduism and Christ", *Logos,* 1969, p. 48.

[62]Panikkar, "...Hinduism and Christ", *Logos,* 1969, p. 48.

[63]Panikkar, "...Hinduism and Christ", *Logos,* 1969, p. 49.

[64]Cf. Panikkar, "...Hinduism and Christ," *Logos,* 1969, p. 50.

[65]Panikkar, "...Hinduism and Christ", *Logos,* 1969, p. 49.

[66]Cf. "Words 'Jesus', 'Christ'" in Menacherry, Cheriyan. *Confluence of Religions, Panikkar's Christological prayāṇa 1,* Chisinau, Moldova: Blessed Hope Publishing, 2022, pp. 26-29.

[67]Panikkar, *The Unknown...,* (1981), p. 164.

[68]Panikkar, *The Unknown...,* (1981), p.56. Cf. Panikkar, *The Unknown...,* (1964), p. 23.

[69]Panikkar *Unknown Christ,* 1981. p. 37.

[70]Panikkar, *Unknown Christ,* 1981. p. 38.

[71]Panikkar, *Unknown Christ,* 1981. p. 38.

[72] Panikkar, *The Unknown...,* (1981), p. 56. "The place of Christ in contrast to any Hindu symbol of the divinity is that the statement we made about Christ makes sense, at least for the Christian, and can be made understandable--if not acceptable--to the Hindu too, whereas a parallel statement about Viṣṇu would not make sense for either of them." Panikkar, *The Unknown...,* (1964), p. 23.

[73]Panikkar states his intention for reinterpreting one of the vedic texts. It is to discover the presence of religious truth in another religion, and this unveiling will be for the mutual enlightenment of all concerned. The discovered truth will be named "by the vocabulary proper to the...tradition recognizing it." If it is by the Christian then he will say "that a 'Christian' truth has been discovered there. In this sense the third part of this book will discover a 'Christian' truth in the Hindu tradition." Panikkar, *The Unknown...,* (1981), p. 7.

[74]"Each time that I speak of Christ I am referring (unless it is explicitly stated otherwise) to the Lord of whom christians can lay claim to no monopoly." Panikkar, *The Trinity...*, (1975), p. 53. Cf. Panikkar, *Intrareligious Dialogue*, (1978), p. 36.

[75]Cf. Panikkar, *The Trinity...*, (1975), p. 53.

[76]Panikkar is not claiming to have solved the problem. "I am not making any claim here to solve the problem, and shall thus continue to use the name of Christ...." Panikkar, *The Trinity...*, (1975), p. 53.

[77]Cf. Panikkar, "Response to Harold Coward," *Cross Currents*, 29 (Summer 1979) p. 192. Cf. Panikkar, *The Trinity...*, (1975), p. 53. Cf. Panikkar, *The Unknown...*, (1981), p.56. Cf. Panikkar, *The Unknown...*, (1964), p. 23.

[78]Panikkar, "Response to H. Coward," *Cross Currents*, (Summer 1979), p. 192. There are "many misconceptions about Christ, perhaps given to Hindus by Christians themselves." Panikkar, *The Unknown...*, (1981), p.56. Cf. Panikkar, *The Unknown...*, (1964), p. 23.

[79]Panikkar is aware of the problem involved in preferring one Christian symbol in the context of meeting of religions. If some find the selection of the name of Christ sectarian, it is "because of the abuses and misunderstanding attached to that name." Panikkar, *The Unknown...*, (1981), p. 6.

[80]Panikkar, "Response to H. Coward," *Cross Currents*, (Summer 1979) p. 192.

[81]Panikkar *Unknown Christ*, 1981. p. 26.

[82]Panikkar *Unknown Christ*, 1981. p. 5.

[83]Panikkar, "Response to H. Coward," *Cross Currents*, (Summer 1979) p. 192.

[84]Panikkar, "Response to H. Coward," *Cross Currents*, (Summer 1979) p. 192.

[85]Panikkar *Unknown Christ*, (1981), p. 27.

[86]Panikkar *Unknown Christ*, 1981. p. 5.

[87]Panikkar *Unknown Christ*, 1981. p. 5.

[88]Panikkar, "Response to H. Coward," *Cross Currents*, (Summer 1979), p. 192.

[89]Panikkar, *Unknown Christ*, (1981), pp. 7-8.

[90]"I...shall thus continue to use the name of Christ, for I believe it is important that the figure of Christ should regain its complete fullness of meaning,..." Panikkar, *The Trinity...*, 1973, p. 53.

[91]"Even by definition the unique link between the created and the uncreated, the relative and the absolute the temporal and the eternal, earth and heaven, is Christ, the only mediator, link, `conveyor', is Christ, the sole priest of the cosmic priesthood, the Lord *par excellence.*" Panikkar, *The Trinity...*, [1970] (1973), p. 53.

[92]Panikkar, *The Unknown...*, (1981), pp. 48-49. "We may be allowed therefore to call Christ that which we consider to be almost by definition the meeting-point, and which at the same time meets the demands of Christian religion." Panikkar, *The Unknown.....*, (1981), pp. 48-49.

[93]Panikkar, "Response to H. Coward," *Cross Currents*, (Summer 1979) p. 192.

[94]Panikkar, *Worship and Secular Man: An essay on the liturgical nature of Man, considering Secularization as a major phenomenon of our time and worship as an apparent fact of all times: A study towards an integral Anthropology,* (London: Darton, Longman and Todd; and New York: Orbis Books, 1973), pp. 76-77.

[95]Panikkar, *Salvation in Christ:..*, (1972), p. 62. "The meaning of Jesus' universality may be even more difficulty to understand in this context [The Lord of History]....The main divergency here does concern Jesus as a symbol for universal salvation, but in the interpretation of salvation itself." Panikkar, *Salvation in Christ:..*, (1972), p. 73.

[96]Panikkar, *The Unknown...*, (1964), p. 45.

[97]Panikkar, *The Unknown...*, (1981), p. 89.

[98]Panikkar, *The Unknown...*, (1964), p. 69. Cf. Panikkar, *The Unknown...*, (1981), p. 101.

[99]Panikkar, *The Unknown...*, (1964), pp. 68-69. Cf. Panikkar, *The Unknown...*, (1981), p. 101.

[100]"In short, the hermeneutical basis for living the Christ myth is not the kind of biblical theology which European Protestants

have been exporting to America these last thirty years or more. It is rather a `Christovidya,‘ informed by the `ontic-intentionality' of a true Catholic encounter with Hinduism." P. Slater, "Hindu and Christian Symbols in the work of R. Panikkar." *Cross Currents* 29 (1979), p. 174. Cf. R. Panikkar, *The Unknown Christ of Hinduism,* (London 1964), 5.

[101]Panikkar, *The Unknown...,* (1964), p. 69. Cf. Panikkar, *The Unknown...,* (1981), p. 101.

[102]Panikkar, "Response to H. Coward," *Cross Currents,* (Summer 1979), p. 190.

[103]Panikkar, "Response to H. Coward," *Cross Currents,* (Summer 1979) p. 191.

[104]Christianity; *Christendom, Church, Christ.* Buddhism; *Sangha, Dharma, Nirvān.a.* Hinduism; *Sampradāya, Karma, Brahman.* Muslim; *Umma, Qur'ān, Allah.* Cf. Panikkar, "Response to H. Coward," *Cross Currents,* (Summer 1979) p. 191.

[105]Panikkar, "Response to H. Coward," *Cross Currents,* (Summer 1979), p. 191.

[106]Panikkar, "Response to H. Coward," *Cross Currents,* (Summer 1979) p. 192.

[107]Panikkar, "Response to H. Coward," *Cross Currents,* (Summer 1979), p. 191.

[108]Panikkar, *The Unknown...,* (1981), p. 27.

[109]"The Son is the mediator, the *summus pontifex* (High Priest) of creation and also of the redemption and glorificationm or transformation of the world. Beings *are* in so far as they participate in the Son, are *from, with* and *through* him. Every being is a *christophany* a showing forth of Christ." Panikkar, *The Trinity...,* p. 54.

[110]Panikkar, *The Trinity...,* (1975), p. 54.

[111]"Wie oft hat mein Hindu=Bruder gemeint, es handle sich um Kṛṣṇa, wenn ich ihm Christus beschreib, und ich antwortete ihm, daß es sicher Christus in Kṛṣṇa sei." Panikkar, *Religionen...,* (1965), p. 17.

FOUR

4 CHRIST: THE LORD AND ĪŚVARA

The main purpose of the entire *Brahma Sūtras* of Bādarāyana[1] is to declare that *Brahman* is the absolute, the supreme principle, the cause of everything, whatever the nature of this *Brahman* might be and whatever degree of reality this world might have.[2] The question is how *Brahman* can relate to the world without losing its absoluteness.[3] The solution is to admit a kind of link which has none of the characteristics of the links we know, except that it somehow connects without fettering down or lifting up the one with the other.[4] There can be seen a difference and unity between *Brahman* and the first cause. They are not the same because one is in `relation-to-the-world`, but at the same time, they refer to the same supreme reality.[5] It is in that situation that the reality *Īśvara* is experienced.[6]

It is well known that in order to defend the absoluteness of Brahman, Śaṅkara's followers were compelled to say that properly speaking it is not Brahman, but *Īśvara* who is the cause of this world, Brahman being completely beyond any kind of relation with this world. Śaṅkara himself in his *bhāsya* leaves the question open. Although in one passage he mentions the word *Īśvara*, he is constantly speaking about Brahman, as the *Sūtras* do. In fact, it is an open question of Śaṅkara's hermeneutics.[7]

On the one hand, there is the immutable *Brahman*, or God, or the Divine Absolute, and there is also this world with all the attributes that cannot be attributed to *Brahman*. On the other hand, there is the world entirely dependent on *Brahman*. It follows that the attributes of the world must proceed from *Brahman*. Yet this raises the question of the immutability of *Brahman*.[8] The same also can be said about the problem of the conservation or return of all things into *Brahman*.[9] If this union is directly with *Brahman*, then the absoluteness of *Brahman* vanishes. The dialectical escape would be to admit a kind of link which does not allow for a perfect communication between the two terms. Otherwise, the characteristics of one term have to be reflected in the other and vice versa, and this reflection would tarnish the very essence of what *Brahman* and the world are supposed to be. This amounts to saying that the link does not really link *Brahman* and the world. There is production and a conservation of the world in a non-temporal, or `eternal' way; and there is also the development or evolution of all these acts, happening concurrently with the temporal development of things. *Īśvara* fulfills both these functions: He "is that from which being is in an `eternal' way; and he is that towards which being tends or be-comes, within the temporal process. This double function of *Īśvara* namely, that one of 'keeping the world in being' in time and 'out of time', is ultimately one, for there are not two worlds, one in eternity and another in time."[10] The expression of the double function of *Īśvara* "attempts to express the non-dualistic intuition of what is otherwise seen as the double 'dimension' of time and eternity. The process is thus tempiternal."[11] This is, in fact, what Śaṅkara and St Thomas Aquinas, among others, have maintained. But even the Advaitic or Thomistic answer that this link is only real from one side, and unreal from the other, does not entirely resolve the difficulty.[12]

A. **Symbol *Īśvara* has Equivalent Function as Symbol Christ**

The relation between *Īśvara* and Christ is not mere comparison[13] or analogy. To explicate the functional equivalence, Panikkar is employing mainly two technical terms homomorphism and homeomorphism. Both are distantly, one can say, enigmatically related.[14] Homomorphism is the functional relation; homeomorphism is topological transformation of a symbol. *Īśvara* and Christ are homologues. Homology is a kind of existential functional analogy. i.e., the notions play equivalent roles, that they occupy homologous places within their respective systems,[15] that means the relationship is homomorphic.[16] The Upaniṣadic concept of *Brahman* and the biblical notion of *Yahweh* are not identical. Still these two concepts have something common. They are homologous, each plays a similar role, albeit in different cultural settings.[17] It is a relation comes by the respective corresponding function in the other system. It represents a functional equivalence discovered through a topological transformation. *Brahman* and God are not merely two analogous names; they are homeomorphic in the sense that each of them stands for something that performs an equivalent function within their respective systems.[18] "The relationship is homomorphic in that the symbol of `God' within one tradition performs an equivalent function to the symbol of `Brahman' in another." Such a view "permits a connection without reducing the uniqueness to sameness or even similarity."[19] "Even more intriguing, perhaps, would be a consideration that homologizes the Indian notion of *Īśvara* (Lord) and the Western idea of Christ.[20]

"Religions do not stand side by side, but they are actually intertwined and inside each other. Vishnu dwells in the heart of Siva and vice-versa. Each religion represents the whole for that particular human group and in a certain way `is' the religion of the other group only in a different topological form."[21] We cannot say one language (religion) is better than the other. In one's language one can express as well as another can in his language.[22]

The symbol of *Īśvara* performs the equivalent function as the symbol of Christ in another tradition.[23] We can say that *Īśvara* and Christ "perform an equivalent function within their respective systems."[24] Panikkar finds a similarity between the functions of the mediating mystery in Hinduism and Christianity.[25]

A. Christ, *Īśvara*: Midpoint between God and World

The midpoint between *Brahman* (God) and the world is *Īśvara*, in the Hindu tradition, and Christ, in the Christian tradition. It is in the philosophical problem of linking *Brahman* and the world[26] "that we find the place of *Īśvara* as well as one of the functions of Christ, in spite of all the differences that can be found between them."[27] The role of *Īśvara* in Vedānta is "to explain the connection between God and the world without compromising the absoluteness of the former or the relativity of the latter-- corresponds functionally of the role of Christ in Christian thought. It is precisely this correspondence that provides Indian philosophy with a locus for Christ and Christian theology for *Īśvara*."[28]

The authors of Hindu scriptures, for instance the Brahmasutras and the commentators did not explicitly think of Christ as they wrote about *Īśvara*. Similarly, the Christ whom the Christians believe cannot be equated with *Īśvara*.[29] Still if one analyses the "`sensus plenior`, a fuller sense" of "mankind's philosophical and theological texts", one arrives "at the `res significata`, the intended thing" of the advaitic *Īśvara* leading to the philosophical possibility of a Christ. It will then open for a higher synthesis between *Īśvara* and Christ.[30] For instance, Panikkar finds the functions of Christ in *Īśvara*, by making a thorough Christological reading of *Brahma Sūtra* I:1:2, "*janmādy asy yataḥ*" "Whence the origin, etc., of this"[31] The scriptural basis of *Brahma-Sūtra* 1.1.2, is *Taittirīya Upaniṣad* III, 1: "That from which truly all beings are born, by which when born they live and into which they are to return: that seek to understand."[32] The *Brahma-Sūtras* represent the quintessence of the *Vedānta*. The second *sūtra* is a cornerstone on which rests a great part of Indian philosophical speculation.[33] This laconic sentence, the most famous summary of Indian Wisdom, is accepted in one form or another by the *Vedānta* and also by the great bulk of Indian philosophy. The universally accepted meaning of the verse is: "Brahman is that from which all things have come forth, in which they are maintained and into which they will return. In one word--also generally accepted--*Brahman is the Cause of the World.*"[34]

For the interpretation, Panikkar does not subscribe neither to Śaṅkara's nor to Rāmānuja. Śaṅkara school's monistic interpretation over stressed the divergence between *Brahman* and *Īśvara* "in order to save the absolute purity of the former."[35] The Rāmānuja school overemphasized the identity between *Brahman* and *Īśvara* "so that somehow *Īśvara* may save the reality of the world, or at least of the *jīvas*, the souls."[36] He uses a new interpretation of non-dualism.[37]

The divine link, the Logos or CHRIST, is the cause of the world. Yet He transcends His causality function and the relationship with the finite, as He has at the same time the transcendental nature of the Father. This CHRIST can also be identified in other religions. Panikkar wants to call this CHRIST by the general term 'Lord'. In the advaitic tradition, this `Lord' is the *Īśvara* of *Vedānta*. But one must not interpret *Īśvara* as is done either by Śaṅkara or Rāmānuja. As mentioned above the "*Īśvara* of the Śaṅkara school is, in fact, almost completely turned towards the phenomenal order. He can still be called God, but is no longer identifiable with the Absolute, with *Brahman*. This *Īśvara* is essentially *saguṇa*, yet somehow claims also to be *nirguṇa*. The divergence between Brahman and *Īśvara* is overstressed in order to save the absolute purity of the former."[38] Rāmānuja's *Īśvara* "is Brahman, and his creation is the Body of the Absolute. In a way, there is no break in continuity between Him and the world. Both together form a whole, the one complete *Brahman*. Here the identity tends to be overemphasized so that somehow *Īśvara* may save the reality of the world, or at least of the *jīvas*, the souls."[39]

Brahma-Sūtra I.1.2 refers not to a *māyā*-affected *Īśvara*, otherwise the gap would subsist and the problem would remain unsolved. *Īśvara*, then, is not merely *saguṇa Brahman*, or an emanation of it, or a mere `modality` of the Godhead. It points to an *Īśvara* who though *saguṇa*, has not ceased to be *nirguṇa*. On the other hand, *Īśvara* "does not belong only to the world of the Godhead. He is not just a mere aspect of the Divine. He is really `human', or rather worldly, without ceasing to be divine." *Īśvara* is God-Man. The *Sūtra* I.1.2 "points towards a reality which not only connects the two poles, but which `is` the two poles without permitting them to coalesce."[40] Thus *Īśvara* "points towards the Mystery of Christ, who, being unique in his existence and essence, is as such equal to God. He is *not* the God, but *equal* to him, Son of God, God from God. Moreover, he has a double nature, but these two natures are `without mixture', and `without change` and yet `inseparable' and `indivisible` (four famous qualifications of the Council of Chalcedon, D 148)." According to Panikkar, CHRIST is more than a mere mediator. He is

the `whole Christ', the whole reality of the world, as far as it is *real*, i.e. as it is--or shall be, if we speak within the framework of time--incorporated in him, one with him, forming one Mystical Body. Thus Christ (*Īśvara*), one with the *real* world[,] is--shall be, if we include time--one with God the Father so that God may be all in all and nothing remain beyond or beside or behind him.[41]

After tracing the functional identity of *Īśvara* and Christ Panikkar concludes his Christological commentary on BS I.1.2. The stages are:

--"That from which truly all beings are born, by which...they live and into which they return: that seek to understand." (TU III, 1). This is the scriptural basis for BS I.1.2.[42]

--*Janmādasya yataḥ*, (Whence the origin 'etcetera' [*sic* et cetera] of this) (BS I,1,2).[43]

--Śaṅkara "interpolates thus: `[Brahman is that] from which the origin [i.e., the origin, subsistence and dissolution] of this [world proceed].'"[44]

Panikkar, as a result of his analysis, began by glossing the text thus:

--*"That from which all things proceed and to which all things return and by which all things are* (sustained in their being) *is God,...."*[45]

Gradually Panikkar's identification of *Īśvara* and Christ grows:

--In 1959: *"That from which this world comes forth and to which it returns and by which it is sustained, that .... that is Christ."*[46]

--In 1964: *"That from which this world comes forth and to which it returns and by which it is sustained, that `that' is Christ."*[47]

--In 1981: *"that from which this world comes forth and to which it returns and by which it is sustained, that is Īśvara, the Christ"* (Cf. Jn 12:32).[48]

"The *place* made in *Vedānta* for *Īśvara, i.e.,* the postulation of *Īśvara* for a role which the philosophical mind finds necessary in order to explain the world and connect God and the World, without compromising the Absoluteness of the former and the Relativity of the latter, that place is filled by Christ in Christian Philosophy. In so far as Christ can be intelligible to Indian Philosophy, as such, it is there that we may find an introductory place."[49] The linkage function (between God and the World) of *Īśvara* in *Vedānta* corresponds to the role of Christ in Christian tradition. "It is precisely this correspondence that provides Indian philosophy with a locus for Christ and Christian theology for *Īśvara.*"[50]*Īśvara* is the only link between the two poles of the absolute and of the relative. This is also one of the functions of Christ as Logos.[51] "The Principle and End of all things has two natures...two faces, two aspects as it were. One face regards the divinity....Another face is turned towards the 'ouside' world."[52] The face turned towards the 'outside' is the *yatha* 'from which' of the *Brahma sūtra.* [53]

C. **CHRIST: *Īśvara* to Hindusm, Logos to Greeks, Messiah to the Hebrews**

It is not by accident or by pure human work that Christ or His functions were reflected in the Hindu scriptures. It was because Christ was present when the rishis composed the *śruti.* Christ has always been at work everywhere. He was present not only when

God created all things, fixing the heavens and commanding the waters, "but also when the Indian rishis composed and handed down the *śruti* for God's wisdom (*sophia, śakti*) `was delighted every day playing before God at all times, playing in the world, for her delight is to be with the children of men'."[54] The unknown presence of Christ had been experienced by Hinduism as the function of relating the world and the Supreme being. The rishis named it *Īśvara*.[55] We can also say that CHRIST made known His name as *Īśvara* to Hinduism, as Logos to the Greeks, as Messiah to the Hebrews.

The names and symbols that different religions attribute to the mediator may not be the same, but all signify the same mystery of the mediator. It is not that reality has many names, as if there were a reality outside the name, but reality is many names; "and each name is a new aspect, a new manifestation and revelation of it. Yet each name teaches or express, as it were, the undivided Mystery."[56] There is no plurality of Christs just as there cannot be a plurality of Gods in the Judaeo-Christian-Islamic conception of God. There is a peculiar link between God and the gods.[57] In the myths of the religions there are different gods or rather God is revealed in different names. Polynomy must not be named as polytheism: "A plurality of God guaranteed by a plurality of names leads to the discovery that there is basic unity among the Gods, that they are, in one way or another, only different manifestations of a single and unique supreme power.... Each name of God does not exhaust the divinity, since there are other names that also refer to the divinity."[58] The Vedic gods are not mere cosmic powers or mere expressions of the human psyche. Nor is there one God with sundry little gods acting as his serving spirits or demons. We may not trace the origins of gods to certain prehistoric powers acting in history in or through the minds and beliefs of different cultural periods. They are not mere subjective factors. The *Gods* are real, in that sense one need not write *gods*, but as *Gods*: "...indeed the gods are not the plural of the monotheistic God. We would have preferred to write simply *devas* for Gods, but the problem of the singular would have remained. Is *deva* God or merely a god? Certainly, it depends on the context. Even then, where does one draw the dividing line between symbols of the divine representing God or one aspect or one name of him and the minor deities which may even include the sense organs? Because of this difficulty, we have decided to keep the ambivalence of the word and write it with a capital letter ...."[59] The *names* of God are the name of *one* God.[60]

So also, there is a subtle relation between the concrete name of the cosmotheandric mystery and the nameless and the utterly transcendent reality itself. Though from different angles and with different understanding, we all 'mean' the 'same'. The relationship, however, between the name and the named, in the above case is deeper than that which exists between a material thing and its nominalistic label.[61] The different understandings of the mystery are not without importance. "Yet both traditions refer to it and the differences should not blur the identity nor-- vice versa."[62]

[1]*Brahma Sūtras* (Vedānta-*Sūtras)* is one of the Sūtras of orthodox *Darśanas,* the authoritative Sūtras of the Vedānta. Cf. J. Helfer, "Brahma Sūtras," in *Abingdon Dictionary of Living Religions,* Gen. Ed. Keith Crim, Tennessee: Abingdon, 1981), p. 117. It is "a summary of attempts by earlier expositors of the teaching of the Upaniṣds. Bādarāyana thus presents *dvaita* Vedānta rather than the purely monistic (*advaita)* doctrine of the early Upaniṣads." Margaret and James Stutley, *A Dictionary of Hinduism: Its Mythology, Folklore and Development 1500 B.C.-A.D. 1500,* (Bombay: Allied Publishers, 1977), p. 53. Cf. also Surendranath Dasgupta, *A History of Indian Philosophy* Vol. I., (Delhi: Montilal Banarsidass, (First ed. Cambridge,1922) 1975), pp. 62, 70. "In a certain sense a whole history of Indian philosophy could be written on the basis of the *Brahma Sūtra bhāsyas.*" Panikkar, *The Unknown...,* (1964), pp. 75-76. Panikkar, *The Unknown...,* (1981), pp. 108-109.

[2]Panikkar, *The Unknown...,* (1964), p. 82. Panikkar, *The Unknown...,* (1981), p.115.

[3]The problem of *Brahman* as the cause of the world--without diminishing his absoluteness on the one hand and the existence

of the world on the other--can be solved neither by dualism nor by pure monism. "This leads us to the almost inevitable paradox, formulated by nearly all theologico-philosophical schools in one way or another: identity and diversity coexist and are both real." Panikkar, *The Unknown...*, (1981), pp. 144-145. Panikkar, *The Unknown...*, (1964), pp. 115-116, cf. pp. 87, 91, 100, 101; cf. also Panikkar, *The Unknown...*, (1981), pp.146, 119, 123, 131-132.

[4]Panikkar, *The Unknown...*, (1964), p. 125.

[5]"This leads us to the almost inevitable paradox, formulated by nearly all theologico-philosophical schools in one way or another: identity and diversity coexist and are both real." Panikkar, *The Unknown...*, (1981), pp. 144-145. Cf. Panikkar, *The Unknown...*, (1964), pp. 115-116. In one sense the cause is identified with *Brahman.* "The First Cause is by definition the ultimate that our knowledge can formally conceive on the metaphysical plane." In both an epistemological and ontological sense the first cause and Brahman are ultimate, so there is kind of identity between *Brahman* and the ultimate cause. Panikkar, *The Unknown...*, (1981), p. 146. Cf. Panikkar, *The Unknown...*, (1964), pp. 115-116. There is also diversity between the First Cause and *Brahman:* "...the First Cause is of a different nature than effects and therefore *something more* than just a *first* being `first` is not a numerical, but a transcendental quality....The reality that is the First Cause is not exhausted in its causal function. This is only its relation-to-the-World, to us: its knowable aspect. Its inmost being, its infinite transcendence, its hidden side is Brahman. Thus there is diversity between the concept of First Cause (as such) and the concept of Brahman. They are not the same, yet they refer to the same Supreme Reality." Panikkar, *The Unknown...*, (1981), pp. 146-147. Cf. Panikkar, *The Unknown...*, (1964), p. 118.

[6]The mystery of *Īśvara* "gives an answer to all the antinomies that the history of Indian Philosophy has found in this mediator between Brahman and the world." Panikkar, *The Unknown...*, (1964), p. 130.

[7]Panikkar, *The Unknown...*, (1964), p. 80. Cf. Panikkar, *The Unknown...*, (1981), p. 112.

[8]Panikkar, *The Unknown...*, (1981), pp. 154-155. Cf. Panikkar, *The Unknown...*, (1964), pp. 124-125.

[9]Panikkar, *The Unknown...*, (1981), pp. 160-161. Panikkar, *The Unknown...*, (1964), p.130.

[10] Panikkar, The Unknown..., (1981), pp. 160 161. Panikkar, The Unknown..., (1964), p.130.

[11] Panikkar, The Unknown..., (1981), pp. 160 161. Panikkar, The Unknown..., (1964), p.130.

[12]Panikkar, *The Unknown...*, (1981), p. 155. Cf. Panikkar, *The Unknown...*, (1964), p. 125.

[13]Panikkar, *The Unknown...*, (1964), p. 68. Cf. Panikkar, *The Unknown...*, (1981), pp. 100-101.

[14] Prateek Joshi, "Homomorphism Vs Homeomorphism" November 16, 2014, https://prateekvjoshi.com/2014/11/16/homomorphism-vs-homeomorphism/#:~:text=So%20technically%2C%20we%20can%20say,homomorphisms%20are%20not%20continuous%20maps.

[15] Panikkar, *Intrareligious Dialogue*, (1978), p.33.

[16] Panikkar, *Intrareligious Dialogue*, (1978), p.33.

[17] Panikkar, *Intrareligious Dialogue*, (1978), pp. 33-34.

[18] Panikkar, Intrareligious Dialogue, (1978), p. xxii.

[19] Panikkar, "Hermeneutics of Comparative Religion: Paradigms and Models." *The Journal of Religious Studies*, VI, (Spring 1978), pp. 48-49.

[20] Panikkar, *Intrareligious Dialogue*, (1978), p. 34. cf. Panikkar, *The Unknown...*, (1964), pp. 119-131.

[21] Panikkar, *Intrareligious Dialogue*, (1978), pp. xxii-xxiii.

[22] Cf. Panikkar, *Intrareligious Dialogue*, (1978), p. xxiv.

[23] Cf. Panikkar, "Hermeneutics of Comparative Religion: Paradigms and Models." *The Journal of Religious Studies*, VI, (Spring 1978), pp. 48-49.

[24]Panikkar, *Intrareligious Dialogue*, (1978), p. xxii.

[25]Panikkar, *The Trinity...*, [1970] (1973), p. 54.

[26]"This subject is the philosophical problem of God and the World--a problem that we discover with our minds and agonize

over in our inner beings." Panikkar, *The Unknown...*, (1981), p. 99. Cf. Panikkar, *The Unknown...*, (1964), p. 67.

[27]Panikkar, *The Unknown...*, (1981), p. 155. Panikkar, *The Unknown...*, (1964), pp. 125-126.

[28] Panikkar, *The Unknown...*, (1981), p. 164. Panikkar, *The Unknown...*, (1964), pp. 133-134.

[29] Panikkar "*Īśvara* and Christ as a Philosophical Problem", *Religion and Society* 6 (1959), pp. 15-16.

[30]Panikkar "*Īśvara* and Christ as a Philosophical Problem", *Religion and Society* 6 (1959), pp. 15-16.

[31] Panikkar, "*Īśvara* and Christ...," *Religion and Society* 6 (1959), p. 9.

[32] Panikkar, *The Unknown...*, (1981), p. 97.

[33] Panikkar, *The Unknown...*, (1981), p. 109.

[34] Panikkar, "*Īśvara* and Christ...," *Religion and Society* 6 (1959), p. 9. Panikkar, *The Unknown...*, (1981), p. 109.

[35] Panikkar, *The Unknown...*, (1981), pp. 158-159. Panikkar, *The Unknown...*, (1964), p. 128.

[36] Panikkar, *The Unknown...*, (1981), p. 159. Panikkar, *The Unknown...*, (1964), p. 129.

[37]"...there is similarity in status and function between *Īśvara* (Lord) in the two modern interpretations of Vedānta <Radhakrishnan and Aurobindo>...and the second person of the Trinity (Logos and Lord) in the theandrism of Panikkar. The reference...is to a divine principle that is linked with the universe, yet is non-different from the Absolute (in accordance with their interpretation of non-difference)." Nalini Devadas, "The Theandrism of Raimundo Panikkar and Trinitarian Parallels in Modern Hindu Thought." *Journal of Ecumenical Studies* 17 (1980), p. 617.

[38]Panikkar, *The Unknown...*, (1981), pp. 158-159.

[39]Panikkar, *The Unknown...*, (1981), p. 159.

[40]Panikkar, *The Unknown...*, (1981), p. 159.

[41]Panikkar, *The Unknown...*, (1981), p. 160. Panikkar, *The Unknown...*, (1964), p. 129.

[42]Panikkar, *The Unknown...*, (1981), p. 97.

[43]Panikkar, *The Unknown...*, (1981), p. 107.

[44]J. Helfer, "Brahma Sūtras," in *Abingdon Dictionary of Living Religions*, Gen. Ed. Keith Crim, Tennessee: Abingdon, 1981), p. 117. Cf. also Panikkar, *The Unknown...*, (1981), p. 107.

[45]Panikkar, *The Unknown...*, (1981), p.155. Panikkar, *The Unknown...*, (1964), p. 126.

[46]Panikkar, "Īśvara and Christ...," *Religion and Society* 6 (1959), p. 15.

[47]Panikkar, *The Unknown...*, (1964), p. 131.

[48]Panikkar, *The Unknown...*, (1981), p. 162.

[49]Panikkar, "Īśvara and Christ...," *Religion and Society* 6 (1959), p. 8.

[50]Panikkar, *The Unknown...*, (1981), p. 164. Cf. Panikkar, *The Unknown...*, (1964), p. 133.

[51] Chethimattam, "...Panikkar's...Christology," *Indian Journal of Theology*, 23 (1974) p. 220.

[52] Panikkar, *The Unknown...*, (1964), p. 127

[53] Chethimattam, "...Panikkar's...Christology," *Indian Journal of Theology*, 23 (1974) p. 220.

[54]Panikkar, *The Unknown...*, (1981), p. 165. Panikkar, *The Unknown...*, (1964), p. 134.

[55] The Vedāntic intuition is not mere rational working but an authentic theological inspiration transmitted by *rishis* and conserved in the *śruti*. That is why we may be allowed to draw upon Scripture. Panikkar, *The Unknown...*, (1981), p. 158. Panikkar, *The Unknown...*, (1964), p.128. Neither the author of the Brahma-Sūtra nor the commentators do intend to write explicitly of Jesus Christ. The "Christ in whom Christians believe cannot be simply equated with the *Īśvara* of the Vedānta." Christianity has always over empahsized the difference--"the newness of the Christian fact, both as revelation and as an ontological `new creation'." Panikkar, *The Unknown...*, (1981), p. 164. Panikkar, *The Unknown...*, (1964), p. 131.

[56] Panikkar, *The Unknown...*, (1981), p. 29.

[57] Panikkar, *The Unknown...*, 1981. p. 6.

[58] Panikkar, "Silence and the Word...," [1969] *Myth, Faith and Hermeneutics*, (1979), pp. 266-267.

[59] Cf. Panikkar, *The Vedic Experience...*, [1977] (1979), p. 11.

[60] Cf. Panikkar, "Silence and the Word...," [1969] *Myth, Faith and Hermeneutics*, (1979), p. 267.

[61] Panikkar, *The Unknown...*, 1981. p. 6.

[62]Panikkar, *The Unknown...*, (1981), p. 51. [not in Panikkar, *The Unknown...*, (1964), cf., p.19.] "It is also an incontrovertible fact that the living Christ in whom Christians believe cannot be equated with the *Īśvara* of Vedānta." Panikkar, "Īśvara and Christ...," *Religion and Society* 6 (1959), pp. 15-16. Panikkar, *The Unknown...*, (1964), p. 132. "...the Christ in whom Christians believe cannot be *simply equated* [my emphasis] with the *Īśvara* of Vedānta." Panikkar, *The Unknown...*, (1981), p. 164.

FIVE

5 The Unknown Christ: Link Between Hinduism and Christianity

The acknowledgement of the presence of Christ in Hinduism[1] gives us a vision of the relation between Hinduism and Christianity, between "the cosmic religions and the religion of his Son."[2] Christianity is not the mere unfolding of a natural religion, there is something new, previously unknown. But the novelty does not cancel out the complementary principle of continuity. [3]

Hinduism is not another religion, another *dharma*, altogether, but a part or stage of the same *sanātana dharma*, -- eternal religion: this is the self-designation of Hinduism which Christianity also claims to be.[4] Hinduism is the concrete expression of the existential *dharma*.[5] Therefore, in the historical unfolding of God's revelation there is a kind of pluralistic continuity held together by what Christians call Christ. Thus, the existential *dharma* of

Hinduism belongs to what Christians call the economy of salvation.[6] This claim is substantiated by Christian faith itself: that God, who has spoken through the prophets and *rishis* (sages),[7] and the expectation of the peoples,[8] "has sent once for all his living and personal Word--one with him--to fulfil all justice, all *dharmas*."[9] This brings a "peculiar dialectic"[10] of Hinduism and Christianity, such as "potency-act, seed-fruit, forerunner-real presence, symbol-reality, desire-accomplishment, allegory-thing in itself."[11] "Hinduism is the starting point of a religion that culminates in Christianity".[12] Hinduism is the precursor.[13] It is Christianity in potency;[14] it already contains "the symbolism of the Christian reality".[15] In Hinduism there is a desire for fulness and that fulness is Christ; and so Hinduism is already pointing towards it.[16] This does not mean that mere natural prolongation will eventually lead from one to the other.[17] The transit is neither a natural nor an automatic one. It is not an immanent evolution.[18] Christianity is not just "a continuation or merely natural prolongation of an earlier religion, but... [it is] the actual new and decisive step towards fullness."[19] Such a decisive step is necessary for Hinduism. The dialectic involved is not merely reducible to the relationship between Old and New covenants.[20] For if Hinduism and Christianity both move in the same direction, yet the transition from one *to* the other implies a conversion, a *pascha*,[21] a mystery of death and resurrection.[22]

A. The Unknown Christ has to be Recognized by Hinduism

Christ is already present in Hinduism. "Hinduism is the desired bride whose betrothal was celebrated long ago in...Vedic times." But she is not yet his spouse.[23] The marriage still remains in the mystery of history.[24] For CHRIST has not unveiled his whole face, has not yet completed his mission in Hinduism. He still has to grow up and to be recognized.[25] Christianity discovers Christ in Hinduism. Christ appears there, "somewhat as a prisoner in a body which still has to die and to rise again, to be converted into `Church` in the precise theological sense of the word."[26] The Christian belief in the mystery of death and resurrection is an example. The Christian "is born a 'pagan' and must first be converted--he must die and rise again in order to become a son of God, a partaker of the divine life."[27] Christ's encounter with Hinduism calls for death. "The Christ that confronts Hinduism presents himself as its death and resurrection."[28] By the work of the *antaryāmin*, the inner guide, which Christians call Christ,[29] Hinduism must "descend into the living waters of baptism in order to rise again transformed".[30] It is this death that Judaism and Hellenistic religions have already experienced. Hinduism is to rise again, "but then as a risen Hinduism, as Christianity. The case of Judaism presents a unique historical feature indeed, but the analogy still holds."[31]

As death is not a total annihilation, conversion is not a total replacement of tradition, or religion. It is a changing into a new life, a new existence, a new creation, which is precisely the old one--and not another--transformed, lifted up, risen again.[32] What will emerge out of the water of death will not be 'another thing, another religion'.[33] For the Christian mystery of resurrection is not an alienation.[34] What emerges from the waters of baptism will be the true Hinduism,[35] a 'better form of Hinduism',[36] consciously acknowledging the CHRIST, the redeemer, the antaryāmin, that was present in it unknown. Then, passing from "the previous limiting beliefs concerning the nature of man,...[Hinduism] will be 'resurrected' in true knowledge of the cosmotheandric reality."[37]

A. **The Mission: Finding the Full Face of Christ**

Christianity also must find the true full face of Christ. Hinduism and Christianity both meet in death.[38] "Christ who is already present in Hinduism and whom Christians can recognize and revere there has not yet completed his mission here on earth, either in Christianity or Hinduism. 'If the grain of wheat does not die...'"[39] The unknown CHRIST, the unknown *reality* which Christians call Christ, is unknown both to Hinduism and to Christianity.[40] So death is needed not only on the part of Hinduism, but also on the part of the present-day Christianity. It is a losing to preserve the real Christian life. It is a death out of the love for the Hindu friends.[41] If by death Hinduism realizes consciously the living presence of the unknown Christ and confesses CHRIST as the Lord, by death Christianity realizes the real, the total, the unknown face of Christ.

This death has a `missionary' motive too. When Christians have found the full and real face of Christ it will be easier for Hindus to acknowledge the same Christ working in them. "The more Christ shines in Christians and in Christianity the easier will it be for Hindus themselves to make the discovery."[42] Of course, Christianity must not undergo a second death, a second baptism. But a special asceticism, a stripping off of all externals, of garb and superficial form, and a lonely vigil with the naked Christ, dead and alive on the Cross is needed.[43] It is with such a *Christian* death, a dying for the friends of other religions, a mystical death that Panikkar himself reached to "the confluence (*sangam*) of the four rivers: the Hindu, Chrisian, Buddhist and Secular traditions."[44]

If the goal of Hinduism is CHRIST and Christianity, it is not the present form of Christianity, or the present image of CHRIST held by Christianity. But it is a perfect Christianity that seeks to embrace the fulness of Christ. In search of this perfection there is a need for the "real mysticism, an immediate contact with Christ which carries the Christian beyond--not against--formulae and explanations. Only then is it possible to discover Christ where he is, for the moment, veiled; only then is it possible to help unveil or reveal the mystery hidden for long ages in God."[45]

C. The Unknown Christ: towards Ecumenical Christophany

When Hinduism and Christianity through `the unknown Christ of Hinduism' come to the understanding of the full Christ, as the cosmotheandric reality,[46] then the `ecumenical Christophany' is achieved. By finding the presence of CHRIST in other religions and at the same time not ascribing to it the name Jesus or Christ,[47] Panikkar avoided calling Jesus, the historical manifestation or symbol of the saving mystery,[48] CHRIST, as universal. And thus, he laid the foundation for ecumenical ecumenism, unity between Hinduism and Christianity without losing their plurality. Now the 'and' between Hinduism and Christianity, passing from mere integration, assimilation or conversion, comes to a higher harmony or, rather, a full symphony. The model for this is the 'and', ambivalent and transcendental, in the Trinity: Father and Son and Holy Spirit.[49]

In the context of ecumenical ecumenism, the ecumenical Christophany, and the unity of Hinduism and Christianity in "the *who* whom Christians see in Jesus",[50] the question of the relation between Jesus and "the only universal Saviour"[51] will be examined in the next issue of the present series.

[1]Cf. Panikkar, *The Unknown...*, (1964), p. 19. Cf. Panikkar, *The Unknown...*, (1981), p. 50.

[2]Panikkar, *The Unknown...*, (1964), p. 59.

[3]"Die ganze christliche Botschaft stellt etwas Neues, vordem Unbekanntes dar, das christliche Ereignis ist eine Mutation in der Geschichte; das Christentum ist nicht die bloße Entfaltung einer naturhaften Religion....Aber die *Neuheit* hebt nicht das ergänzende Prinzip der Kontinuität auf." R. Panikkar, "Eine Betrachtung über Melchisedech," *Kairos* 1 (1959) p. 10.

[4]Cf. Panikkar, *The Unknown...*, (1964), p. 19. *Dharma* does not mean `religion', "as this latter word implies a sociological reality...." Panikkar, *The Unknown...*, (1981), p. 50. Dharma means "Cosmic order, right, duty, religious law, social and religious observences handed down by tradition; 'religion' regarded as a set of practices and laws. That which holds the world together. One of the four 'human goals' (*puruṣārtha*)." Panikkar, *The Vedic Experience...*, [1977] (1979), p. 876.

[5]Cf. Panikkar, *The Unknown...*, (1964), p. 19. Panikkar, *The Unknown...*, (1981), p. 50.

[6]Panikkar, *The Unknown...*, (1981), p. 50.

[7]Panikkar, *The Unknown...*, (1964), p. 19. Cf. Panikkar, *The Unknown...*, (1981), p. 50.

[8]Cf. Panikkar, "...über Melchisedech," *Kairos* 1 (1959), p. 10.

[9]Panikkar, *The Unknown...*, (1981), p. 50-51, 89. Hebrew 1:1. Cf. Panikkar, *The Unknown...*, (1964), p. 19.

[10]Panikkar, *The Unknown...*, (1964), p. 58

[11]Panikkar, *The Unknown...*, (1981), p. 71, also p. 90.

[12]Panikkar, *The Unknown...*, (1964), p. 58. "Das Christentum ist nicht einfach eine andrere Religion. Es ist die Religion und die Erf`llung aller Religionen." Panikkar, "...über Melchisedech," *Kairos* 1 (1959), p. 14.

[13]Cf. Panikkar, "...über Melchisedech," *Kairos* 1 (1959) p. 13.

[14]Cf. Panikkar, *The Unknown...*, (1964), p. 59.

[15]Panikkar, *The Unknown...*, (1964), p. 60. Cf. Panikkar, *The Unknown...*, (1981), p. 90.

[16]Panikkar, *The Unknown...*, (1964), p. 60. Panikkar, *The Unknown...*, (1981), p. 90.

[17]Panikkar, *The Unknown....*, (1964), p. 58.

[18]Panikkar, *The Unknown...*, (1964), p. 60.

[19]Panikkar, *The Unknown...*, (1981), p. 90.

[20]Panikkar, *The Unknown....*, (1964), p. 58.

[21]Panikkar, *The Unknown...*, (1964), p. 58.

[22]Panikkar, *The Unknown...*, (1964), p. 60; cf. pp. 17-18.

[23]Panikkar, *The Unknown...*, (1964), pp. 17-18.

[24]Panikkar, *The Unknown...*, (1964), p. 18.

[25]Panikkar, *The Unknown...*, (1964), p. 17.

[26]Panikkar, *The Unknown...*, (1964), p. 18.

[27]Panikkar, *The Unknown...*, (1964), p. 18.

[28]Panikkar, "...Hinduism and Christ", *Logos*, 1969, p. 51.

[29]Panikkar, *The Unknown...*, (1981), p. 93.

[30]Panikkar, *The Unknown...*, (1964), p. 60.

[31]Panikkar, *The Unknown...*, (1964), p. 17.

[32]Panikkar, *The Unknown...*, (1964), p. 18.

[33]Panikkar, *The Unknown...*, (1964), p. 60.

[34]Panikkar, *The Unknown...*, (1964), p. 60.

[35]Just as "the true Aristotle is that of thirteenth century," as St Thomas Aquinas tried to explicate what is in the philosophy of Aristotle. Panikkar, *The Unknown...*, (1981), p. 167.

[36]Panikkar, *The Unknown...*, (1964), p. 61.

[37]Panikkar, *The Unknown...*, (1981), pp. 93-94.

[38]Cf. Panikkar, *The Unknown...*, (1964), p. 18. Panikkar, *The Unknown...*, (1981), p. 49.

[39]Panikkar, *The Unknown...*, (1981), p. 50.

[40]Cf. Panikkar, *The Unknown...*, (1981), pp. 20-20. "In such a dialogue of religions neither party has the last word. For the Christian the life-enhancing power and liberating vision engendered by the exchange will be the true word, the Unknown Christ. But this will be a Christ not fully known by either party beforehand." Slater, "Hindu & Christian Symbols...," *Cross Currents* 29 (Summer 1979), p. 181.

[41]"Der Preis dafür aber ist der Tod - als notwendige Voraussetzung der Auferstehung -, aber nicht nur der der anderen und der anderen Religionen, sondern auch und vor allem der "eigene", d.h. der des gegenwärtigen Christentums. Es steht doch geschrieben, nicht nur, daß, wer sein Leben erhalten will, es verlieren wird, sondern auch, daß niemand mehr Liebe hat als der, der sein Leben für seine Freunde hingibt. Wir nennen uns aber Freunde...." Panikkar, *Kerygma und Indien:...* (1967), pp. 9-10.

[42]Panikkar, *The Unknown...*, (1964), p. 61.

[43]Panikkar, *The Unknown...*, (1981), p. 59.

[44] It seems that Panikkar himself had such death, the mystical experience when he lost his fellow traveller when he reached his ancesteral dwelling. When he began his journey to different lands there was a fellow traveller. "Child of my own time and environment, I thought I knew well who that companion was in my intellectual and spiritual wonderment of over a half-century ago. There came however, a critical moment when I reached my

ancestral dwelling-place at the peak-period of my life: my companion disappeared....Risking my life in offering my services to everybody without accepting their respective dialectics, I found myself suddenly in the World of Times. And from there the sacredness of everything, even of the secular, dawned upon me. Thus I am at the confluence (*sangam*) of the four rivers: the Hindu, Chrisian, Buddhist and Secular traditions." Panikkar, *The Unknown...,* (1981), pp.ix-x.

[45]Panikkar, *The Unknown...,* (1981), p. 59.

[46]Panikkar, *The Unknown...,* (1981), p. 94.

[47]"In other religions he may not be recognized as Jesus and yet the real and not only the nominal link to the transcendent is...the Christ." (Panikkar, "...Christ unique?" *Theoria to Theory,* (1967), p. 131.) In non-Christian religions "Christ is not explicitly acknowledged as the Lord." (Panikkar, "...`non-Christians'," *Cross Currents* 22 (1972), p. 282.) That which holds everything; that in which every man in one or other form believes--that [is] the mediator (whatever name we may give to it). Panikkar, "...Christ unique?" *Theoria to Theory,* (1967), p. 131.

[48]Panikkar, *Salvation in Christ:...,* (1972), p. 71.

[49]Panikkar, *The Unknown...,* (1981), p. 96.

[50]Panikkar, *Salvation in Christ:...,* (1972), p. 72.

[51]Panikkar, *Salvation in Christ:...,* (1972), p. 72.

Bibliography

(The comprehensive bibliography has also been compiled with a view to the forthcoming books in the *Panikkar's Christological prayāṇa* series. The bibliography is divided into three parts: A. Primary Source: Panikkar's bibliography, has been divided into 1st books and 2nd articles [arranged chronologically]. B. Secondary source: the literature related to Panikkar, has been divided into 1. books/articles and 2. book reviews. C. Other sources: Books and articles consulted).

A. Primary source: The Bibliography of Panikkar

1. Books

1948

________. *F.H. Jacobi y la Filosofía del sentimiento*. Buenos Aires: Sapientia, 1948.

1949

________. *Actas del Congreso Internacional de Filosofía. Barcelona, 1948*, Consejo Superior de Investigaciones Científicas, Madrid, 1949, 3 vols, ed., R. Panikkar.

1951

________. *El Concepto de Naturaleza: Análisis Histórico y Metafísico de un Concepto*. Consejo Superior de Investigaciones Científicas, Madrid, 1951. Second Edition, Madrid: C.S.I.C., 1972.

1960

________. *La India: Gente, Cultura, Creencias*. Madrid: Rialp, 1960.

--In Italian: *L'India: Popolazione cultura e credenze*. Morcellina: Brescia, 1964.

--In French: *Lettre sur l'Inde*. Tournai: Casterman, 1963.

1961

________. *Patriotismo y Cristiandad*. Madrid: Rialp, 1961.

________. *Ontonomía de la ciencia. Sobre el sentido de la Ciencia y sus relaciones con la Filosofía*. Madrid: Gredos, 1961.

1963

________. *Humanismo y Cruz*. Madrid: Rialph, 1963.

__________. *L'incontro delle religioni del mondo contemporaneo: Morfosociologia dell'ecumenismo.* Roma: Edizioni Internazionali Sociali, 1963.

__________. *Die vielen Götter und der eine Herr: Beitrage zum Ökumenischen Gespräch der Weltreligionen.* Weilheim/Oberbayern: Otto Wilhelm Barth, 1963.

--In Spanish: *Los dioses y el Seen~or.* Buenos Aires: Columba, 1967.

1964

__________. *Religione e Religioni. Concordanze Funzionale ed Esistenziale delle Religioni. Studio Filosofico sulla natura storica e dinamica della religione.* Brescia: Morcelliana, 1964.

--In Spanish: *Religión y religiones.* Madrid: Gredos, 1965.

--In German: *Religionen und die Religion* München: Max Hüber, 1965.

__________. *The Unknown Christ of Hinduism.* London: Darton, Longman and Todd, 1964.

-English reprint, London: Darton, Longman & Todd 1968.

-English reprint, London: Darton, Longman & Todd 1977.

--(For the revised and enlarged edition see below under 1981.)

--In German: *Christus der Unbekannte im Hinduismus.* Luzern & Stuttgart: Räber, 1965.

--In Spanish: *El Cristo desconocido del Hinduismo.* Madrid: Marova & Barcelona: Fontanella, 1970.

--In French: *Le Christ et l'hindouisme: Une présence cachée.* Paris: Centurion, 1972.

--In Italian: *Il Cristo sconosciuto dell'Induismo.* Milano: Vitae Pensiero, 1975.

-Some parts also in *Māyā e Apocalisse. L'incontro del'Induismo e del Christianesimo.* Roma: Abete, 1966. pp. 133-164, 291-357.

__________. *Kultmysterium in Hinduismus und Christentum: Ein Beitrag zur vergleichenden Religionstheologie.* Freiburg & München: Karl Alber, 1964.

--In French: *Le Mystère du Culte dans l'Hindouisme et le Christianisme.* Paris: Cerf, 1970.

--Extract in German published as: "Aktion und Kontemplation im indischen Kultmysterium", *Una Sancta* (1966) p.145-150.

1966

_________. *Māyā e Apocalisse: L'incontro del'Induismo e del Christianesimo*. Roma: Abete, 1966.

--In Spanish: *Misterio y Revelación: Hinduismo y Cristianismo: Encuentro de dos Culturas*. Madrid: Marova, 1971.

--also in "Christus und Indien, Jesus und Wir", *Kairos* X (1968) pp. 115-132.

1967

_________. *Kerygma und Indien. Zur heilsgeschichtlichen Problematik der christlichen Begegnung mit Indien*. Hamburg: Herbert Reich, 1967.

_________. *Offenbarung und Verkundigung: Indische Briefe*. Freiburg: Herder, 1967.

_________. *Técnica y Tiempo. La Tecnocronía*. Buenos Aires: Columba, 1967.

1968

_________. *La Gioia Pasquale*. Vicenza: La Locusta, 1968.

1969

_________. *L'Homme qui devient Dieu. La foi dimension constitutive del'homme*. Paris: Aubier, 1969.

--In French "La Foi Dimension Constitutive de l'homme", *Archivio di Filosofia:Mito e Fede*, 34 (1966) pp. 17-44.

--Also as: "Faith as a Constitutive Human Dimension", in *Myth, Fith and Hermeneutics. Cross Cultural Studies*. New York: Paulist press, 1979, pp. 187-229.

1970

_________. *La presenza di Dio*. Vienza: La Locusta, 1970.

_________. *El Silencio del Dios. Un mensaje del Buddha al mundo actual: Contribución al estudio del ateísmo religioso*. Madrid: Guadiana, 1970.

--In Italian: *Il silenzio del Buddha*. Roma: Nuova Borla Editrice, 1984.

--Re-elaborated in Italian: *Il Silenzio di Dio: la Risposta del Buddha.* Roma, 1985.

--Also in English: "The Silence of the word: Non dualistic polarities." *Cross Currents* 24, 2-3 (Summer/Fall, 1974) pp. 154-171.

--Also as *The Silence of God: The Answer of the Buddha.* New York: Orbis Books, 1989.

__________. *The Trinity and World Religions. Icon-Person-Mystery.* Madras: The Christian Literature Society, 1970.

--*Revised and published as: The Trinity and the Religious Experience of Man: Icon-Person-Mystery.* London: Darton, Longman and Todd, 1973.

--Reprint: London: Darton, Longman and Todd; and New York: Orbis Books, 1975.

--Some parts in *Spiritualità indù: Lineamenti.* Brescia: Morcelliana, 1975.

--Also in *Kerygma und Indien. Zur heilsgeschichtlichen Problematik der christlichen begegnung mit Indien.* Hamburg: Herbert Reich, 1967. pp. 101-138.

--Also in "Towards an Ecumenical Theandric Spirituality", *Journal of Ecumenical Studies,* 5 (Summer 1968) 507-534.

1972

__________. *Dimensioni Mariane della Vita.* Vicenza: La Locusta, 1972.

--An extract published as: "The Marian Dimensions of Life", *Epiphany* 4 (Summar 1984) pp. 3-9.

__________. *Cometas: Fragmentos de un diario espiritual de la postguerra.* Madrid: Suramérica, 1972.

__________. *Salvation in Christ: Concreteness and Universality; The Supername.* Santa Barbara, 1972.

--Also in "The Meaning of Christ's name in the Universal Economy of Salvation," in *Documenta Missionalia 5: Evangelization Dialogue and Development,* (Selected papers of the International Theological Conference: `International Theological Congress on Evangelization' Nagpur India October, 1971. Dhavamony ed., (Roma 1972) pp. 195-218.

1973

________. *Worship and Secular Man: An essay on the liturgical nature of Man, considering Secularization as a major phenomenon of our time and worship as an apparent fact of all times: A study towards an integral Anthropology.* London: Darton, Longman and Todd; and New York: Orbis Books, 1973.

--Reprint: London (DLT) and New York: Orbis Books 1975.

--In French: *Le culte et l'homme séculier.* Paris: Seuil, 1976.

--In Spanish: *Culto y secularización: Apuntes para una antropología liturgica.* Madrid: Marova, 1979.

1975

________. *Spiritualità indù: Lineamenti.* Brescia: Morcelliana, 1975.

1977

________. *The Vedic Experience. Mantraman~jari^: An Anthology of the Vedas for Modern Man and Contemporary Celebration.* London: Darton, Longman and Todd, (1977) reprint 1979.

--Revised Indian edition: Pondicherry: All India Books, 1983.

1978

________. *The Intrareligious Dialogue.* New York: The Paulist Press, 1978.

-Indian edition: Bangalore: Asian Trading Corporation, 1984.

--In French: *Le dialogue intra-religieux.* Paris: Aubier, 1984.

--In Polish: Warszawa: Instytut Wyadawniczy PAX, 1985.

1979

________. *Myth, Faith and Hermeneutics: Cross Cultural Studies.* New York: The Paulist Press, 1979.

-Indian edition: Bangalore: Asian Trading Corporation, 1983.

--In German: *Rückkehr zum Mythos* aus. Eng. Bettina Bäumer. Frankfurt: Isel Verlag, 1985.

- revised edition, US: Paulist Press 1999.

1981

________. *The Unknown Christ of Hinduism: Towards an Ecumenical Christophany.* Revised and enlarged ed., London: Darton, Longman & Todd; and New York: Orbis Books, 1981.

-Indian Edition: Bangalore: Asian Trading Corporation, 1982.

--In German: *Der unbekannte Christus im Hinduismus* Mainz: Matthias Grünewald, 1986.

--(For the first ed., see above under 1964).

1982

__________. *Blessed Simplicity: The Monk as Universal Archetype.* (In dialogue with E. Cousin, C. Tholens, M. Dardenne, A.Veilleux, M.B. Pennington & P. Soleri). New York: Seabury Press, 1982.

1993

__________ *The Cosmotheandric Experience: Emerging Religious Consciousness* edited by Scott Eastham. Maryknoll, N.Y. Orbis Books, 1993.

-------------- *A Dwelling Place for Wisdom.* Louisville, Kentucky Westminster John Knox Press, 1993

1995

-------------- *Invisible Harmony: Essays on Contemplation and Responsibility* edited by Harry James Cargas. Minneapolis: Augsburg Fortress Publishers,1995

__________ *Cultural Disarmament: The Way to Peace.* Louisville, Kentucky Westminster John Knox Press; 1995

2004

__________ Christophany: The Fullness Of Man. Mary Knoll: Orbis Books, , 2004.

2006

__________ The Experience of God: Icons of the Mystery (trans. by Joseph Cunneen). Fortress Press, 2006.

__________ Initiation to the Vedas. India: Motilal Banarsidass, , 2006

2009

__________ The Rhythm of Being. The Gifford Lectures. Mary Knoll Orbis Books, 2009,

2. Articles

1942

__________. "Investigación." *Revista de Filosofía,* no., 2 & 3, Consejo Superior de Investigaciones Cientificas, Madrid, 1942, pp. 389-398.

1944

_________. "Los productos químicos: su intervención en la curtición de las pieles." *Piel* 9/10, Madrid, 1944, pp. 72-75.

_________. "Visión de Síntesis del Universo." *Arbor: Revista General de la Investigación y la Cultura* 1 (Jan- Feb., 1944) pp. 5-40.

_________. "La Ciencia Biomatemática: Un Ejemplo de Síntesis Científica." *Arbor: Revista General de la Investigación y la Cultura* 1 (May-June 1944) pp. 349-372.

1945

_________. "El indeterminismo científico." *Anales de Física y Química* 41 (1945) p. 396.

_________. "El Sentido cristiano de la Vida. Su Aspecto Paradigmático en los primeros cristianos." *Arbor: Revista General de la Investigación y la Cultura* 4 (September - Octorber 1945) pp. 261-282.

-also in *Humanismo y Cruz* (Madrid 1963) 121-152.

1946

_________. "El sentido químico: de la industria de la piel." *Piel* - 29, Madrid (1946) pp. 11-16.

1947

_________. "Max Planck (1858-1947)." *Arbor: Revista General de la Investigación y la Cultura* 8 (Nov-Dece 1947) pp. 387-406.

_________. "F.H.Jacobi y la Filosofía." *Sapientia* 2 (1947) pp. 322-343; and 3 (1948) pp. 23-59.

--Also published as: "F.H.Jacobi y la Filosofía del Sentimiento." *La Ciencia* 13 (1948) pp. 157-224.

--Also as: *F.H.Jacobi y la Filosofía del Sentimiento* (Buenos Aires 1948).

1948

_________. "De Deo Abscondito." *Arbor: Revista General de la Investigación y la Cultura* 9 (1948) pp. 1-26.

--Also in *Humanismo y Cruz* (Madrid 1963) pp. 254-290.

1949

________. "La unidad física de tiempo." *Communication au Congreso International de Filosofia,* (Barcelone, 4 - 10 Oct., 1948) Madrid, 1949.

1950

________. "El Atomo de Tiempo." *Arbor: Revista General de la Investigación y la Cultura.* 15 (January 1950) pp. 1-32.

1951

________. "Etiquetas Cristianas y realismo teológico en nuestra Cultura." *Arbor: Revista General de la Investigación y la Cultura* 18 (1951) pp. 595-597.

--Also published as: "Sobre el Sentido Cristiano de la Vida." in *Humanismo y Cruz* (Madrid 1963) pp. 112-162.

________. "El Cristianismo no es un Humanismo." *Arbor: Revista General de la Investigación y la Cultura* 18 (1951) pp. 165-186.

--A revised and condensed version in *Sapientia* 6 (1951) pp. 135-140.

________. "El Miedo Intelectual y la prudencia de la carne." *Arbor: Revista General de la Investigación y la Cultura* 19 (1951) 532-534.

--Also in *Humanismo y Cruz* (Madrid 1963) pp. 116-121.

________. "La Novedad que en el Concepto de Naturaleza introduce el Cristianismo." in *Tijdschrift voor Philosophie* 13 (June 1951) pp. 236-262.

________. "Una cautela a los historiadores espan~oles." *Arbor: Revista General de la Investigación y la Cultura* 19 (1951) 532-534; and 20 (1951) pp. 112-113.

________. "El Dinamismo de la Naturaleza." *Giornale di Metafisia* 6 (1951) 155-167.

________. "La Naturaleza en la Ciencia Físico-Metemática." *Sapientia* 6 (1951) 36-46.

1952

________. "Cristianidad y Cruz. Una Investigación Teológico-Histórica." *Arbor: Revista General de la Investigación y la Cultura* 19 (1951) 532-534; and 23 (1952) pp. 337-367.

--Also in *Humanismo y Cruz* (Madrid 1963) pp. 291-334.

________. "La Eucaristía y la Resurreción de la Carne: Texto de la Comunicación al Congreso Eucarístico Internacional de Barcelona, May 1952." in *Humanismo y Cruz* (Madrid 1963) pp. 335-352.

________. "Introduction." In Guitton Jean, *La Virgen Maria* (Madrid 1952) pp. 30-34.

________. "Sind die Katholiken Katholisch? Das Corpus und seine Glieder." In *Wort und Wahrheit*, 7, Freiburg (1952) pp. 649-655.

1953

________. "Le concept d'ontonomie." in Proceedings of the XIth. International Congress of Philosophy Bruxelles 20-26 August 1953, *Metaphysics and Ontology* Vol., III. Louvain: Nauwelaerts, 1953. pp. 182-188.

________. "La Evolución del Patriotismo en Occidente." *Sapientia* 8 (1953) pp. 283-293.

________. "Honorabilidad Intelectual." *Arbor: Revista General de la Investigación y la Cultura* 24 (1953) pp. 316-324.

________. "Réflexions sur les réunions internationales de catholiques." *Pax Romana* (1953) pp. 3-5.

________. "Sobre la Teología y la Universidad." *Revista de Educación* 12 (1953) pp. 79-82.

--A modified version in *Humanismo y Cruz* (Madrid 1963) pp. 90-111.

________. "El Sujeto del Patriotismo." *Revista de Teología* 3 (1953) pp. 28-37.

1955

________. "Freiheit und Gewissen." *Neues Abendland*, 1, München, (1955) pp.25-32.

________. "Das Vaterland der Christen." *Neues Abendland* 10 (1955) 131-138.

________. "Extra Ecclesiam nulla salus. Die innere Unzulängklichkeit einer nicht- christischen Welt." *Neues Abendland* X, 5, München, May 1955, pp. 259-266.

--In Spanish: "Extra Ecclesiam nulla Salus", in *Humanismo y Cruz* (Madrid 1963) 163-177.

__________. "Die Sünde der Intellektuellen." *Neues Abendland* 10 (1955) pp. 643-648.

1956

__________. "Letter to a Christian Artist." *All India Study Week,* (June 13, Madras 1956) pp. 119-127.

--Also published as: "Letter to an Indian Christian Artist." *Liturgical Art* 32 (November 1963) pp. 9-12.

__________. "Sur l'anthropologie du prochain." In *L'Homme et son prochain: Actes du 8ème Congrès des Sociétés de Philosophie de Langue Française, Toulouse, Septembre 6-9, 1956.* Paris: Presses Universitaires de France, 1956, pp. 229-231.

__________. "Christian Meaning and Human Values." *The King's Rally* 33 (1956) pp. 25-32.

__________."Die Existentielle Phänomenologie der Wahrheit." in *Philosophisches Jahrbuch der Görres Gesellschaft* 64 (1956) pp. 27-54.

--"The Existential Phenomenology of Truth." *Philosophy Today* 2 (Spring 1958) pp. 13-21.

--In Italian: "La fenomenologia esistenziale della veritá," in *Māyā e Apocalisse. L'incontro del'Induismo e del Christianesimo.* Roma: Abete, 1966, pp. 241-289.

__________. "If God exists." *Vedanta Kesari* (December 1956).

--in *The Unknown Christ of Hinduism.* London: Darton, Longman and Todd, 1964. pp. 70-73.

--in *The Unknown Christ of Hinduism: Towards an Ecumenical Christophany.* London: Darton, Longman & Todd; and New York: Orbis Books, 1981. pp. 102-105.

1957

__________. "Does Indian Philosophy need Re-orientation? The recovery of its theological background for the reorientation of Indian Philosophy." *Philosophy East and West* (April 1957) pp. 23-28.

--In Italian: "L'Esigenza di un Nuovo Orientamento della Filosofia indiana." in *Māyā e Apocalisse. L'Incontro dell'Induismo e del Cristianesimo.* Roma: Abete, 1966, pp. 33-69.

_________. "Mission of the Laity in the Church." *The King's Rally* (Madras) 34 (1957) pp. 123-129.

_________. "The Sanctity of St. John of the Cross and of St. Theresa." in *Prabuddha Bharata*, III (1957) pp. 1-6.

--Also published as: "Some aspects of Spirituality of St. John of the Cross and of St. Theresa." *The Living Word* 76 (November - December 1970) pp. 258-268.

_________. "Some Phenomenological Aspects of Hindu Philosophy Today." *Oriental Thought* 3 (1957) pp. 151-191.

--Also published as: "Contemporary Hindu Spirituality." *Philosophy Today* 3 (Summer 1959) pp. 112-127.

-- In German, "Aspekte heutiger Hindu-Spiritualität." (trans, by Heiler A.M.), in Heiler A.M. ed., *Inter Confessiones: Beiträge zur FÖrderung des Interkonfessionellen und Interreligiösen Gesprächs Friedrich Heiler zum Gedächtnis aus Anlass seines 80 Geburtstage am 30.1.1972* (Marburg 1972) pp. 132-153.

1958

_________. "The Theological Basis for Christian-non-Christian co-operation in Social Thought and Action," *Religion and Society* 5 (March 1958) 29-36.

--In Italian: "Basi Teologiche per una cooperazione attiva fra Cristiani e non Cristiani." in *Māyā e Apocalisse: L'Incontro dell'Induismo e del Cristianesimo*. Roma: Abete, 1966, pp. 175-184.

_________. "The Integration of Indian Philosophical and Religious Thought." *Religion and Society* 5 (June 1958) 23-29.

--A modified version: "Indian Philosophy and Christian Doctrine." *Frontier* (October 1958) pp. 271-274.

--In Spanish: "La integración del pensamiento filosófico y religioso de la India." *Orbis catholicus*, 7 (Barcelona 1960) pp. 1-7.

-Also in *Criterio* 36 (Buenos Aires, 1963) pp. 247-248.

--In French: "Integration de la Pensée philosophique et religieuse de l'Inde." *Bulletin du Cercle Saint Jean-Baptiste* 20 (February 1963) pp. 16-22.

--In Italian: "Il Problema della integrazione del Pensiero filosofico e religioso indiano nella teologia." in *Māyā e Apocalisse: L'incontro dell'Induismo e del Cristianesimo.* Roma: Abete, 1966 pp. 165-173.

1959

_________. "Ishwara and Christ as a Philosophical Problem." *Religion and Society* 6 (1959) pp. 8-16.

--Also published as "The Is'vara of Vedānta and the Christ of the Trinity as Philosophical Problem." in *Atti del XII Congresso Internatizonale di Filosofie (Venezia 12-18 Settembre 1958) Vol., X: no., 50: Filosofie Orientali e Pensiero Occidentale* (Firenze 1960) pp. 153-160.

--In German: "Der Ishwara des Vedanta und der Christus der Trinität. Eine Philosophisches Problem." *Antaios* 2 (1961) pp. 446-455.

--Also in *The Unknown Christ of Hinduism.* London: Darton, Longman and Todd, 1964. pp. 126-131.

--Also in *The Unknown Christ of Hinduism: Towards an Ecumenical Christophany.* London: Darton, Longman & Todd, and New York: Orbis Books, 1981, pp. 155-162.

_________. "Eine Betrachtung über Melchisedech." *Kairos* 1 (1959) pp. 5-17.

--Also in *Melchisedech: Urgestalt der ökumene.* Freiburg: Herder 1979.

--In Italian: "Meditazioni su Melchisedech." in *Māyā e Apocalisse. L'Incontro dell'Induismo e del Cristianesimo.* Roma: Abete, 1966, pp. 185-203.

--"Christ Abel and Melchizedek: The Church and the nonAbrahamic religions." *Jeevadhara*, V (Sep-Oct., 1971) pp. 391-403.

_________. CUTTAT J.A. *Vergeistingungs'Technik' und Umgestalltung in Christus,* (Comment), *Kairos* 1 (1959) pp. 18-30; 2 (1960) pp. 44-45.

_________. `The Symbol He is'. Contribution to *Swami Parama Arubi Anandam* (Fr Monchanin. A memorial), Tiruchirappalli: Saccidanda Ashram, 1959, pp. 127-131.

1960

________. "Keine christlicher Yoga, aber Yoga ist eine nochoffene christliche Propädeutik." *Kairos* 2 (1960) pp. 44-45.

________. "Um das Religiöse Gespräch." *Kairos* 2 (1960) p. 180.

________. "Konferenzen der `Pax Romana' in Manila 26.12.1959 bis 8.1.1960." *Kairos* 2 (1960) pp. 106-107.

________. "The Brahman of the Upaniṣads and the God of the Philosophers." *Religion and Society* 17 (Sept., 1960) no., 2. pp. 12-19.

--In German: "Das Brahman der Upaniṣaden und der Gott der Philosophen." *Kairos* 3 (1961) 1/2 pp. 182-188.

1961

________. HACKER P., *Magie, Gott Persona und Gnade im Hinduismus* (Comment) in *Kairos* 2 (1960) pp. 225-233; 3 (1961) pp. 112-114.

________. "La Demitolgizzazione nell'incontro del Cristianesimo e l'Induismo." *Archivo di Filosofia: Il Problema della Demitizzazione.* (Padua: Cedam, 1961) pp. 243-266.

--In Spanish: "El Encuentro con la India", in *Los Dioses y el Sen~or* (Buenos Aires 1967) pp. 45-67.

________. "Nota al Padre Dhanis", *Achivio di Fisosofía* 19 (1961) pp. 333-334.

________. "La espiritualidad hindú", *Nuestro Tiempo* 8 (October 1961) pp. 1181-1207.

________. "Eucharistischer Glaube und Idolatrie." *Kairos* 3 (1961) pp. 85-90.

________. "Hinduismus und Magie", *Kairos* 3 (1961) pp. 112-114.

________. "Pluralismus, Toleranz und Christenheit." in *Pluralismus, Toleranz und Christenheit*, Hans Schomerus (u.a); Nürnberg: Abendländische Akademie, 1961, pp. 117-142.

--Also in "Tolerance, ideology and Myth." Panikkar, *Myth, Faith and Hermeneutics.* New York: The Paulist Press, 1979, pp. 20-33.

--In Spanish: in *Los Dioses y el Sen~or* (Buenos Aires 1967) pp. 116-146.

________. "La Tempiternidad. La Misa como `Consecratio Temporis'." In *Sanctum Sacrificum: Proceedings of the 'V Congreso*

Eucarístico Nacional'. Zaragoza (1961) pp. 75-93.

_______."Hinduism and Christianity." in *Student World,* LV, 3 (Genève, 1963) pp. 304-323.

--Also in *Cross Currents,* XIII (1963) pp. 87-101.

--In French: "Hindouisme et christianisme." *Mitte me* 5 (1963) pp. 1-9.

1962

_______. "Le Fondement du Pluralisme Herméneutique dans l'hindouisme." *Demitizzazione e Immagine.* Padua: Cedam, 1962, pp. 243-259.

--In Spanish: *Los Dioses y el Sen~or.* Buenos Aires 1967, pp. 67-97.

--In German: "Die Begründung des hermeneutischen Pluralismus in Hinduismus." *Kerygma und Mythos: Entmythologisierung und Bild.* VI, Band II, Hamburg: Herbert Reich, 1964.

_______. "Letter to a Christian Student of Hinduism." *Logos* (Colombo) 3 (October 1962) pp. 1-5.

_______. "Forme e crisi della spiritualità contemporanea." *Studi Cattolici,* no., 33, (Roma, June, 1962) pp. 9-23.

_______. "Spätantiker Heidentum (Comments)." by Raimundo Panikkar and E. von Ivanka in *Kairos* 4 (1962) pp. 83-90; 5 (1963) pp. 69-70.

_______. "Zur Einführung in die indische Weltanschauung." In *Stimmen der Zeit* 170. Bd. 87. (Freiburg 1962) pp. 177-185.

--in English: "Indian Philosophy, an Introduction", *Philosophy Today* 8 (Summer 1964) pp. 110-117.

1963

_______. "Sur l'herméneutique de la Tradition dans l'hindouisme. Pour un Dialogue avec le Christianisme." in *Archivio di Filosofia: Ermeneutica e Tradizione* 31 (Paris: Vrin; and Roma: Istituto die studi filosofici, 1963) pp. 342- 364.

--In Italian: "Sull'ermeneutica della Tradizione nell'Induismo. Per un dialogo con il Christianesimo", *Humanitas* 19 (1964) pp. 953-983.

--"The Hermeneutics of Hermeneutics. Reflections on the hermeneutics of Tradition in Hinduism in view of a dialogue with Christian thought." *Philosophy Today* 2 (Fall 1967) pp. 166-183.

--In German: "Über die Hermeneutik der Tradition im Hinduismus", in *Kerygma und Indian: Zur heilsgeschichlichen Problematik der christlichen Begegnung mit Indien* (Hamburg 1967) pp. 67-90.

__________. "La Metafísica de los textos hindués sobre la creación." *Atlántida* 1 (Jan. - Feb. 1963) pp. 86-90.

__________. "Progresso Scientifico e Contesto Culturale: Discussion." Raimundo Panikkar and others, *Civiltá delle Macchine* (May - June 1963) pp. 19-29.

__________. "Panikkar Raimundo, "Una Meditazione teologica sulle tecniche di Comunicazione", *Studi Cattolici* 7 (1963) pp. 11-16.

--In Spanish: "Una consideración teológica sobre los medios de comunicación social." *Atlántida* 1/4 (Jul.-Aug. 1963) pp. 435-441.

__________. "El espíritu religioso del pueblo castellano." *Nuestro Tiempo* (Sep. 1963) pp. 3-16.

__________. "Sugerencias para una Teofísica." *Convivium* 21 (1966) pp. 235-243.

--in Italian: "Introduzione alla Teosofica." *Civiltá delle Macchine*, Roma (Nov. 5, 1963) pp. 28-32.

__________. "Communication sur l'Inde face à l'athéisme de l'Occident." in Veuillot P., Henry A. M., and others, eds., *L'Athéisme, Tentation du Monde, Réveil des chrétiens?* Paris: Cerf, 1963, pp. 53-57.

__________. "La Confidencia. Análisis de un sentimiento." in *Rivista Espan~ola de Filosofía*. Madrid: Consejo Superior de Investigaciones Científicas, 1963, pp.43-62.

__________. "Der Zerbrochene Krug, zur indischen Symbolhaftigkeit," *Antaios* 4 (1963) pp. 556-571.

--Also in *Kultmysterium in Hinduismus und Christentum. Ein Beitrag zur vergleichenden Religionstheologie.* Freiburg & München: Karl Alber, 1964, pp. 135-146.

__________. "Europa und die Frage nach der kulturellen Einheit der Menschheit," in *Das Europänische Erbe in der Heutigen Welt.*

Edited by Walter Werr. Nürnberg: Abendländishe Akademie E.V., 1963.

1964

________. "Technique et Temps: la Technochronie", *Archivio di Filosofia: Tenica e Casistica.* 32 (1964) pp. 195-229.

--An extract: "Technology and Time, Technochrony", *Pax Romana Journal* (February 1967) pp. 3-6.

________. "Das erste Bild des Buddha. Zur Einführung in den buddhistischen Apophastismus", *Antaios* 6 (1964) pp. 373-385.

--In Italian: "La Prima Immagine del Buddha. Per una introduzione all'apofatismo buddhista", *Humanits* 21 (June 1966) pp. 608-622.

--In German: "Das erste Bild des Buddha", in *Kerygma und Indian: Zur heilsgeschichlichen Problematik der christlichen Begegnung mit Indien.* Hamburg: Herbert Reich, 1967, pp. 91-100.

1965

________. "Morale du Mythe et Mythe de la Morale: Mythologie et Logomythologie." *Archivio di Filsosofia: Demitizzazione e Morale* 33 (Aubier-Montaigne, 1965) pp. 393-413.

--"Morality and Myth. The Moral of Myth and the Myth of Morals." In *Myth, Fith and Hermeneutics: Cross Cultural Studies.* New York, Ramsey, Toronto 1979, pp. 37-64.

________. "Advaita and Bhakti, Lettera da Vrindaban", *Humanits* 20 (1965) pp. 991-1001.

--In German: "Die Begegnung indischer Weisheit mit christlicher Liebe", in *Kerygma und Indian: Zur heilsgeschichlichen Problematik der christlichen Begegnung mit Indien.* Hamburg: Herbert Reich, 1967, pp. 59-65.

--"Advaita and Bhakti. A Letter from Vrindaban." in *Bhagawan Das Commemoration Volume* (Varanasi 1969).

--Also "Advaita e Bhakti, love and identity in a Hindu Christian Dialogue." *Journal of Ecumenical Studies* 7 (Spring 1970) pp. 299-309.

--Also in *Myth, Faith and Hermeneutics.* New York: The Paulist Press, 1979, pp. 277-289.

--Also in *Revista de Occidente,* no., 91 (1970) pp. 38-52.

________. "Letter from Holy Mount Athos." *Sobornost*, IV, no., 12, (1965) pp. 726-731.

--In French: "Lettre du Saint mont Athos." *Christus* 12 (July 1965) pp. 418-424.

________. "Relation of Christians to their non-Christian Surroundings." *Indian Ecclesiastical Studies* 4 (July - August 1965) pp. 303 - 348.

--Also in Joseph Neuner, ed., *Christian Revelation and World Religions*. London: Burns and Oates, 1967, pp. 143-184.

--Also published as: "Christians and so-called 'non-Christians'." *Cross Currents* 22 (Summer-Fall 1972) pp. 282-308.

--Also in D.J. Elwood, ed., *What Asian Christians are Thinking. A Theological Source Book*. Quezon City, 1976, pp. 339-376.

--In German "Das Verhältnis der Christen zu ihrer nicht-christlichen Welt." in *Kerygma und Indian: Zur heilsgeschichlichen Problematik der christlichen Begegnung mit Indien*. Hamburg, 1967, pp. 29-58.

1966

________. "L'Eglise et les Religions du Monde." *Orient* 8 (1966) pp. 7-15.

--Italian: "La Chiesa e le religioni del mondo." (trans by M. Riccati Di Ceva), *Humanitas*, (Brescia, Feb.-March, 1966) pp. 168-173.

--"Church and the World Religions." *Religion and Society*, XIV, Nr. 2 (Bangalore, 1967) pp. 59-63.

________. "Hinduism / Christianity", (Excerpt from *The Unknown Christ of Hinduism*. London: Darton, Longman and Todd, 1964). *Jubilee* 13, (Jan. 1966) pp. 28-33.

________. "La Foi Dimension Constitutive de l'homme", *Archivio di Filosofia:Mito e Fede*, 34 (1966) pp. 17-44.

--Also published as: *L'Homme qui devient Dieu: La foi dimension constitutive de l'homme*. Paris, 1969.

--"Faith - A Constitutive Dimension of Man", *Journal of Ecumenical Studies* 8, no., 2 (Spring 1971) pp. 223-254.

--Also as: "Faith as a Constitutive Human Dimension", in *Myth, Faith and Hermeneutics. Cross Cultural Studies*. New York: Paulist press, 1979, pp. 187-229.

__________. "The Crisis of Madhyamika and Indian Philosophy Today." *Philosophy East and West* 16 (1966) pp. 117-131.

--In Italian: "La Crisi della Filosofia Indiana." in *Māyā e Apocalisse: 'Incontro dell'Induismo e del Cristianesimo*. Roma: Abete, 1966, pp. 99-130.

__________. "Philosophen-Kongress in Indien", *Kairos* 8 (1966) p. 67.

__________. "Philosophy and Theology: Reason and Faith - An Essay in Terminological Clarification." in *The Concept of Philosophy* (Banaras s. d.) pp. 507-534.

--In Italian: "L'Esigenza di un nuovo orientamento della Filosofia indiana." in *Māyā e Apocalisse L'Incontro dell'Induismo e del Cristianesimo*. Roma: Abete, 1966, pp. 33-69.

__________. "La Problematica dell'aggiornamento Monastico." in *Visioni Attuali sulla Vita Monastica*. Montserrat, 1966, pp. 221-230.

--"The Problem of Monastic Aggiornamento", *The Monastic Studies* (1969) pp. 103-112.

__________. "Aktion und Kontemplation im indischen Kultmysterium", *Una Sancta* (1966) pp. 145-150. [Extract of the book: *Kultmysterium in Hinduismus und Christentum. Ein Beitrag zur vergleichenden Religionstheologie*. Freiburg & München: Karl Alber, 1964.]

1967

__________. "La faute originante, ou l'immolation créatrice: le mythe de Prajapati." *Archivio di Filosofia: Il Mito della Pena*, 35 (1967) pp. 65- 100.

--Also as "La faute originante." *Le mythe de la peine*. Aubier-Montaigne, Paris, 1967.

--"The Myth of Prajapti. The originating Fault or Creative Immolation", in *Myth, Faith and Hermeneutics*. New York: The Paulist Press, 1979, pp. 65-95.

__________. "Intervention." in A. Caracciolo, "Le Mal dans l'experience religieuse." *Archivio di Filosofia: Il Mito della Pena*, 35 (1967) pp. 265-281.

__________. "Intervention." in S. Lyonnet, "La Problématique du Péché originel dans le Nouveau Testament." *Archivio di Filosofia: Il Mito della Pena*, 35 (1967) pp. 101-120.

__________. "The European University Tradition and the Renascent World Cultures: A Challenge to the European University." *Geneva, World councils of Churches: Christian presence in higher Education.* Basal, 1967, pp. 72-87.

--Also in *Communio Viatorum* (January - February 1968) pp. 1-15.

__________. "Dialogue between Ian and Ray: Is Jesus Christ unique?" Raimuno Panikkar and Ian Stephens, *Theoria to Theory*, I (Jan., 1967) pp. 127-137.

1968

__________. "Herméneutique de la liberté de la religion. La Religion comme liberté." *Achivio di Fisosofia: L'ermeneutica della Liberté Religiosa*, edited by Castelli 36 (Paris: Aubier-Montaigne, 1968) pp. 57-86.

--"Hermeneutics of Religious Freedom: Religion as Freedom." in *Myth, Faith and Hermeneutics*. New York: The Paulist Press, 1979, pp. 419- 460.

--In German: "Hermeneutik der religiösen Freiheit: Die Religion als Freiheit, in *Kerygma und Mythos*, VI, Band V, Hamburg: Herbert Reich, 1974, pp. 118-136.

__________. "Intervention", in RICOEUR P. "Approche Philosophique du Concept de Liberté religieuse." *Achivio di Fisosofia: L'ermeneutica della Liberté Religiosa*, edited by Castelli 36 (Paris: Aubier-Montaigne, 1968) pp. 253-252.

__________. "The God of Being and the `Being' of God: An Exploration", *Harvard Divinity Bulletin* (Spring 1968) pp. 12-16.

--A modified version: "God of Silence." *Indian Journal of Theology* XXI (Jan-Jun., 1972) pp. 116-124.

--Also as: "The God of being and the `Being' of God. Religion and Atheism", in *Myth, Faith and Hermeneutics*. New York: The Paulist

Press, 1979, pp. 349-360.

--Also in *El Silencio del Dios. Un mensaje del Buddha al mundo actual: Contribución al estudio del ateísmo religioso.* Madrid: Guadiana, 1970.

_______."The Internal Dialogue--The Insufficiency of the so-called phenomenological `Epoché' in the Religious Encounter," *Religion and Society* XV, 3. (1968) pp. 55-66.

--Also in *The Intra-Religious Dialogue.* New York: Ramsey, 1978, pp. 39-52.

_______. "Ogni autentica Religione e via di salvezza." In *Incontro tra le religioni, Doucmenti Nuovi.* Roma: Mondadori (1968) pp. 107-123.

_______. "Religionwissenschaft oder Religionsgeschihte?" *Kairos* 10 (1968) pp. 56-57.

_______. "Towards an Ecumenical Theandric Spirituality." *Journal of* Ecumenical *Studies* 5 (Summer 1968) pp. 507- 534.

--In German: "Idolatrie, Personalismus, Advaita", in *Kerygma und Indian: Zur heilsgeschichlichen Problematik der christlichen Begegnung mit Indien.* Hamburg, 1967, pp. 101-138.

--also in *The Trinity and World Religions: Icon. Person. Mystery.* Madras: The Christian Literature Society, 1970.

_______. "Christus und Indien, Jesus und Wir." [Ein Gespräch in Rom über *Māyā e Apocalisse. L'incontro del'Induismo e del Christianesimo,* von Raimundo Panikkar, Roma: Abete, 1966.] X *Kairos* (1968) pp. 115-132.

1969

_______. "Le Silence et la Parole. Le Sourire du Bouddha." Achivio *di Fisosofia L'Analisi del Linguaggio Teologico Il Nome di Dio* 37 (1969) pp. 121-134.

--In Spanish: "La Sonrisa de Buda", *La Revista de Occidente* 76 (July 1969).

--Revised version in English: "Nirvāna and the Awareness of the Absolute." in J.P. Whelan, ed., *The God Experience: Essays in Hope: The Cardinal Bea Lectures, Vol., II.* New York, Toronto: Newmann Press, 1971, pp. 81-99.

--Again: "Nirvāna and The Awareness of the Absolute." *Dialogue* 9 (Colombo 1982) pp. 104-120.

--Again as: "Silence and the Word. The Smile of the Buddha", in *Myth, Faith and Hermeneutics.* New York: The Paulist Press 1979 pp. 257-276.

__________. "Confrontation between Hinduism and Christ", *New Blackfriars* 50 (January 1969) pp. 197-204.

--Also in *Logos* (Colombo) 10 (1969) pp. 43-51.

__________. "The Alternative. A Kairological Meditation on the All India Seminar on the Church in India." *The Examiner* (Bombay, April 12, 1969) pp. 229-230 and continued in *The Examiner* (Bombay, April 19, 1969) pp. 245-246.

--In Italian: "L'Alternativa. Meditazione Kairologica sulla conferenza panindiana e sulla Chiesa in India." *Humanitas* 24 (December 1969) pp. 1141-1153.

__________. "Metatheology or Diacritical Theology as Fundamental Theology". In *Concilium* (Nijmegen) VI, no., 5 (June 1969) pp. 21-27.

--Also in *Myth, Faith and Hermeneutics.* New York: The Paulist Press, 1979, pp. 321-334.

__________. "An open letter to Mr. Shusaku Endo on his book `The Silence'." *The Japan Missionary Bulletin* XXIII (November 1969) pp. 623-624.

__________. "La Présence de Dieu." *La Vie Spirituelle* (December 1969) pp. 527-533.

__________. "Christianity and the World Religions." In *Christianity* [Collective work]. Patiala: Punjabi University (1969) pp. 78-127.

__________. "The People of God and the Cities of Man." Setphen Verney, ed., *The People and Cities.* London: Collins, Fontana Books, 1969, pp. 190-219.

__________. "Zero." *Frontier* 12 (1969) pp. 252-254.

--In German: "Die Null: Ungestalt des Nichts." in J. Tenzler, ed., *Urbild und Abglanz. Beiträge zu einer Synopse von Weltgestalt und Glaubenswirklichkeit* (Regensburg 1972) pp. 175-178.

________. "Algunos aspectos de la espiritualidad hindú," in, L. Sala Balust and Jiménez Duque (eds) *Historia de espiritualidad*. Barcelona: Flors, 1969, pp. 433-542.

--In Italian: *Spiritualità indù: Lineamenti*. Brescia: Morcelliana, 1975.

1970

________. "Le Sujet de l'Infaillibilité. Solipsisme et Vérification." *Archivio di Filosofia: L'Infallibilità, L'aspetto Filosofico e Teologico*. 38 (1970) pp. 423-445.

--In Spanish: "El Sujeto de la infalibilidad." *Revista de Occidente* 108 (March 1972).

--"The Subject of Infallibility. Solipsism and Verification" in *Myth, Faith and Hermeneutics*. New York: The Paulist Press, 1979, pp. 389-417.

--In German: "Das Subjekt der Unfehlbarkeit. Solipsismus und Verifikation" in *Kerygma und Mythos VI: Aspect der unfehlbarkeit Kritische Untersuchungen und Interpretationen* edited by Dr. Franz Theunis, Lüwen/Belgien, Hamburg: Herbert Reich, 1975, pp.178-193.

________. "Je crois." *Parole et Mission*. Paris, Cerf, 50 (May-1970) pp. 258-260.

________. "Machines and Men." *Frontier* 13 (June 1970) pp. 258-260.

________. "Indirect Methods in the Missionary Apostolate: Some Theological Reflections." In *Indian Journal of Theology* 19 (Jul-Dec., 1970) pp. 111-113.

________. "Buddhismo è Ateismo?" in *L'Ateismo Contemporaneo*, Vol., IV: *Il Cristianesimo di fronte all'Ateismo* (Torino 1970) pp. 449-476.

________. "Cristianismo y Culturas." *Diccionario Salvat*. Barcelona, 1970, pp. 12-13.

________. "Fe y Creencia. Sobre la Experiencia multireligiosa." in *Homenaje a Xavier Zubiri* Vol., 2. (Madrid: E'ditorial Moneda y Crédito, 1970) pp. 435-459.

--A shortened and revised version in English: "Faith and Belief: A Multireligious Experience. An Objectified Autobiographical

Fragment." *Anglican Theological Review.* III, no., 4 (October, 1971) pp.219-237.

--Also in *The Intra-Religious Dialogue.* New York, 1978, pp. 1-23.

__________."Menneskehedens enhed menneskehedens Splittelse." *Nordisk Missions-Tidsskrift* I, no., 81. Copenhaguen (1970) pp. 92-98.

__________. "Secularization and Worship." in Von Bussum, ed., *Worship and Secularization* (Amsterdam 1970) pp. 28-71.

--Also in *Studia Liturgica* 7 (1970) pp. 28-71.

__________. "The Ultimate Experience: The Ways of East and West." in G. Devine, ed., *New Dimensions in Religious Experience: Proceedings of the XVI Annual Convention of the College Theology Society.* New York: Alba House, Staten Island, 1970, pp. 69-93.

--A revised version in *Indian Ecclesiastical Studies* 10, no., 1, (January, 1971) pp. 18-39.

--Also published as: "The Supreme Experience: The Ways of East and West," in *Myth, Fith and Hermeneutics: Cross Cultural Studies.* New York: The Paulist Press, pp. 291-317.

__________. "Die Zukunft kommt nicht später." in L. Reinisch, ed., *Vom Sinn der Tradition.* München: C.H. Beck, 1970, pp. 53-64.

__________. "The Myth of Incest as Symbol for Redemption in Vedic India." In *Types of Redemption: Contributions to the Thema of the Study Conference held at Jerusalem--14ᵗʰ to 19ᵗʰ July, 1968.* ed. by R.J. Zwi Werblosky and C. Jouco Bleeker. London: E.J.Brill, 1970, pp. 130-143.

__________. "La Alternativa: Meditación Kairológica sobre un seminario panindio que estudie la situación de la Iglesia en la India." In *Convivium,* no., 32 (1970) pp. 3-14.

1971

__________. "Die Philosophie in der geistigen Situation der Zeit." in *Akten des XIV. Internationalen Kongress für Philosophie, Wien 2-9 Sept. 1968.* Vienna: Herder, 1971, pp. 75-87.

--also as "The Philosophical Tradition." in *Myth, Faith and Hermeneutics.* New York: The Paulist Press, 1979, pp. 335-348.

__________. "La loi du Karma et la dimension historique de l'Homme." *Archivo di Filosofia: Ermeneutica e Escatologia,* 39 (1971) pp.

205-230.

--"The Law of karman and the historical dimension of man", *Philosophy East and West* 22 (1972) pp. 25-43.

--Also in *Myth, Fith and Hermeneutics. Cross Cultural Studies.* New York: The Paulist Press, 1979. pp. 361-388.

__________. "Il messagio dell'India di ieri al mondo di oggi" *Filosofia*, no., I (January, 1971) pp. 3-28.

--"The Message of Yesterday's India to Today's World." *Religion and Society* 27 (1981) pp. 64-74.

__________. "Indology as a Cross-Cultural Catalyst. A New Task of Indological Studies: Cross-Cultural Fertilization." *Numen*, 18 (Dec. 1971) pp. 173-179.

__________. "Die Fata Morgana der Zukunft." *Una Sancta* 26 (1971) pp. 212-218.

--"The Mirage of the Future." *Teilhard Review* VIII, no., 2. London (June-1973) pp. 42-45.

__________. "Der Mythos der Zukunft." in *Zukunft der Theologie. Theologie der Zukunft.* Vienna, Freiburg, Basel: Herder, 1971, pp. 17-26.

__________. "Philosophy of Religion in the Contemporary Encounter of Cultures." in R. Klibansky, ed., *Contemporary Philosophy: A Survey.* Firenze: La Nuova Editrice, 1971, pp. 221-242.

__________. "The Relation of the Gospels to Hindu Culture Religion." in D. G. Miller, D. Y. Hadidian, eds., *Jesus and Man's Hope*, Vol., II. Pittsburgh 1971, pp. 247-261.

__________. "The Rules of the Game in the Religious Encounter." *The Journal of Religious Studies*, III (Spring 1971) pp. 12-16.

--Also in *The Intrareligious Dialogue.* New York: The Paulist Press, 1978, pp. 25-37.

--Also in Gerald H. Anderson and Stransky, Thomas F., *Mission Trends No., 5: Faith Meets Faith: Lively Opinions from four Continents about Christian witness in the encounter with people of other faiths.* New York: Paulist Press, 1981. pp. 111-122.

--In French: "Quelques Présupposés à la Rencontre des Religions." *Rhythmes du Monde* 19 (1971-72) pp. 27-31.

--Also in *Diotima* 6 (1978) pp. 102-107.

1972

_______. "Témoignage et dialogue." *Archivo di Filosofia: La Testimonianza*, 40 (1972) pp. 367-388.

--"Witness and Dialogue", In *Myth, Fith and Hermeneutics: Cross Cultural Studies.* New York, Ramsey, Toronto 1979. pp. 231-256.

_______. "Some Aspects of Suffering and Sorrow in the Vedas." *Jeevadhara* II, no., 11 (Sept. - Oct., 1972) pp. 387-398.

--Also as: "Physical ailment." in *The Vedic Experience. Mantraman~jarí: An Anthology of the Vedas for Modern Man and Contemporary Celebration.* London: Darton, Longman and Todd, (1977) reprint, 1979, section I, part IV.

_______. "Súnyatā and Pléróma: The Buddhist and Christian Response to the Human Predicament." *Religion and the Humanizing of Man: Plenary Addresses, International Congress of Learned Societies in the Field of Religion.* Canada: Waterloo, 1972, pp. 67-86.

--Also in *The Journal of Religious Studies* VI, no., 1 (Spring 1978) pp.16-34.

_______. "Prolegomena to the Problem of the Universality of the Church." in J.B. Chethimattam, ed., *Unique and Universal: Fundamental Problems of an Indian Theology.* Bangalore: CSWR, Dharmaram 1972, pp. 155-163.

_______. "The Theandric Vocation." *Monastic Studies* no., 8 (Spring-1972) pp. 67-74.

--In Portuguese: "A Vocaçãso Teândrica. Santidade: Afirmaçâo e Depojamento." *Grande Sinai* 33 (1979) pp. 205-213.

_______. "`Super hanc petram': Due Principi Ecclesiologici: La Roccia e Le Chiavi." in *Legge e Vangelo: Discussione su una legge fundamentale per la Chiesa.* Paideia, 1972, PP. 135-145.

_______. "The Meaning of Christ's name in the Universal Economy of Salvation." In *Documenta Missionalia 5: Evangelization Dialogue and Development.* Roma, 1972, pp. 195-218.

--And in *Salvation in Christ: Concreteness and Universality, the Supername.* Santa Barbara, 1972, pp. 16-41.

--Also in Joseph Patrapankal, ed., *Service and Salvation*, Bangalore: Theological Publications in India, 1973, pp. 235-263.

1973

__________. "Tolérance, Idéologie et Mythe." *Archivo di Filosofia: Demitizzazione e Ideologia* 41 (1973) pp. 191-206.

--"Tolerance, Ideology and Myth", In *Myth, Fith and Hermeneutics: Cross Cultural Studies*. New York, Ramsey, Toronto, 1979, pp. 19-36.

--In Spanish: "Tolerancia, ideologíe y mytho." *Dialogos*, no., 79 (México) (January - February 1978) pp. 4-10.

__________. "The Category of Growth in Comparative religion: A Critical Self-examination. In *Harvard Theological Review* 66, No 1 (January 1973) pp. 113-140.

--Also in *The Intrareligious Dialogue* (New York: The Paulist Press, 1978) pp. 53-78.

__________. "Philosophy and Revolution: The Text, the Context and the Texture." *Philosophy East and West*, 3 (July, 1973) pp. 315-322.

__________. "Apologie de la Scolastique." *Diogène*, no., 83 (Jul-Sept., 1973) pp. 105-118.

__________. "Action and Contemplation as Categories of Religious Understanding." in *Main Currents in Modern Thought* 30 (Nov.-Dec., 1973) pp. 75-81.

--Also in *The Indian Journal of Theology* 15 (January-March 1976) pp. 17-29.

--Also in Y. Ibish and I. Masculescu, eds., *Contemplation and Action in World Religions. Selected Papers from the Rothok Chapel Colloquium on `Traditional Modes of Contemplation and Action'*. Seattle, London: A Rothko Chapel Book, 1978 pp. 85-104.

__________. "Monólogo con Vicente Fatone." In *Obras Completas de Vicente Fatone*. Vol., II, Buenos Aires, Suramericana, 1973, pp. 195-218.

__________. "Vāc in the S'ruti", In G. Gispert-Sauch, ed., *God's Word Among Men: Papers in Honour of Fr Joseph Putz, S.J., Fr J. Bayrt, S.J., J. Volckaert,S.J. and P. De Letter, S.J.* New Delhi: Vidiyajyoti Institute of Religious Studies, 1973, pp. 3-24.

1974

__________. "Le mythe comme Histoire Sacrée: Shunahshepa, un Mythe de la Condition Humaine." *Archivo di Filosofia: Il Sacro* 42 (1974) pp. 243-315.

--" S'una̠hs'pa. A Myth of the Human Condition," In *Myth, Fith and Hermeneutics: Cross Cultural Studies.* New York: The Paulist Press, 1979. pp. 97-184.

__________. "Have the `Religions' the *Monopoly* on Religion? Editorial." *Journal of Ecumenical Studies* XI, no., 3 (Summer 1974) pp. 515-517.

__________. "The Hindu Ecclesial Consciousness. Some Ecclesiological Reflections" *Jeevadhara* XXI (May-June, 1974) pp. 199 - 205.

__________. "The Silence of the Word: Non-dualistic Polarities." *Cross-Currents* 24 (Summer/Fall, 1974) pp. 154-171.

__________. "The Monk according to the Indian Sacred Scriptures." *Cistercian Studies* 9 (1974) pp. 253-255.

__________. "Toward a Typology of Time and Temporality in ancient Indian Tradition." *Philosophy of East and West* 24 (1974) pp. 161-164.

--Also in *Journal of Ecumenical Studies* XXIV (April, 1974) pp. 161-164.

1975

__________. "El presente tempiterno. Una apostilla a la historia de la salvación y a la teología de la liberación." in *Teología y Mundo Contemporáneo. Homenaje a K. Rahner en su 70 cumpleaños* Madrid 1974. Edited by A. Vargas Machuca. Madrid: Universidad Pontificia de Comillas, 1975, pp. 133-175.

In: "Le Temps Circulaire: Temporisation et Temporalité." *Archivo di Filosofia: Temporalità e Alienazione* 43 (1975) pp. 207-246.

__________. "La Visione Cosmoteandrica: Il Senso religioso emergente del terzo millennio." in R. Caporale, ed., *Vecchi e Nuovi Dei: Studi e Riflessioni sul senso religioso emergente degli Atti del Il Simposio Internazionale sulla Credenza, organizzata dalla Fondazionale sulla Credenza, organizzata dalla Fondazione Giovanni*

Agnelli a Vienna 7-11 Gennaio 1975. Valentino: Torino 1976, pp. 521-544.

--"The Cosmo theandric Vision: An Emerging consciousness for the Third Millennium A.D." *Vecchi e Neuoni Dei*, edited by R. Caporale. Torino: Valentino, 1976 pp. 521-544.

________. "The Contribution of Christian Monasticism in Asia to the Universal Church" *Cistercian Studies* 10, no., 2 (1975) pp. 73-74.

________. "Seed-Thoughts in Cross-Cultural Studies: Pensées dans la problématique pluriculturelle." *Monchanin* VIII, 3-5, cahier 50, (June- December, 1975) pp. 1-73.

________. "Astrologie." *Monchanin* VIII, 3-5, cahier 50 (Jun-Dec., 1975) pp. 71-73.

________. "Cross-Cultural Studies." *Monchanin* VIII, 3-5, cahier 50, (June- December, 1975) pp. 12-15.

________. "Le Dialogue." *Monchanin* VIII, 3-5, cahier 50, (June-December, 1975) pp. 47-50.

________. "Ecology from an Eastern Philosophical Perspective." *Monchanin* VIII, 3-5, cahier 50, (Jun-Dec., 1975) pp. 23-28.

________. "Education Religieuse dans une perspective inter-religieuse." *Monchanin* VIII, 3-5, cahier 50, (Jun-Dec., 1975) pp. 51-70.

________. "The Emerging Myth." Preface to Jacques Langlais, *Le Bouddha et les bouddhismes*, (Montreal 1975).

--Also in *Monchanin* VIII, 3-5, cahier 50, (Jun-Dec., 1975) pp. 8-11.

________. "L'Est et l'Ouest." *Monchanin* VIII, 3-5, cahier 50, (June-December, 1975) pp.37-45.

________. "Myth in Religious Phenomenology." *Monchanin* VIII, 3-5, cahier 50, (Jun-Dec., 1975) pp. 16-17.

________. "Mythos et Logos." *Monchanin* VIII, 3-5, cahier 50, (June-December, 1975) p. 46.

________. "Religious Education in an Inter-Faith Perspective." *Monchanin* VIII, 3-5, cahier 50, (Jun-Dec., 1975) pp. 23-32.

________. "Symbols and Reality. The 'Symbolic' Difference." *Monchanin* VIII, 3-5, cahier 50, (Jun-Dec., 1975) pp. 18-22.

________. "Inter-Religious Dialogue: Some Principles (Editorial)." *Journal of Ecumenical Studies* 12 (Summer 1975) pp. 407-409.

________. "Eastern and Western Ways of Thinking about God." (An interview between Panikkar and Walter T. Brennan, O.S.M), *Listening* 10 (Winter 1975) pp. 78-83.

________. "The Mutual Fecundation." (Foreword to) in T. Paul, ed., *The Emerging Culture in India.* Alwaye: Pontifical Institute of Theology and Philosophy, 1975, pp. 9-11.

________. "Singularity and Individuality. The Double Principle of Individuation." *Revue Internationale de Philosophie*, XXIX, no., 111-112, fasc. 1-2 (1975) pp. 141-166.

________. "Some Notes on Syncretism and Eclecticism related to the growth of human consciousness." in B.A. Pearson, ed., *Religious Syncretism in Antiquity. Essays in conversation with Geo. Widengren* (Montana 1975) pp. 47-62.

________. "Temps et Histoire dans la Tradition de l'Inde:" *Les Cultures et les Temps.* -- UNESCO-- Paris: Payot, 1975, pp. 73-101.

________. "Verstehen als Überzeugtsein" in H.G. Gadamer and P. Vogler, *Neue Anthropologie*, Vol., 7 *Philosophische Anthropologie*, Zweiter teil. Stuttgart: Georg Thieme Verlag, 1975, pp. 132- 167.

1976

________. "La Sécularisation de l'herméneutique. Le Cas du Christ: Fils de l'Homme et Fils de Dieu." *Archivo di Filosofia: L'Ermaeneutica della Secolarizzazione.* 44 (Padua, cedam, 1976) pp. 213-248.

--In German: "Die Säkularisierung der Hermeneutik. Der Fall Christus: Menschensohn und Gottessohn," in *Kerygma und Mythos VI - 9: zum problem der Sékularisierung ; Mythos oder Wirklichkeit Verhängnis oder Verhei$ung?* (Von) E. Grassi, P Ricoeur etc. (Akteu des Colloquiums über "Die Hermeneutik der Säkularisierung" Roma, Januar 1976 unter dem vorsitz von Enrico castelli). Hamburg -Bergstedt: H. Reich, 1977, pp. 141-165.

________. "Prologue." in A.T. de Nicolas, *Avatar and the Humanization of Philosophy through the Bhagavad Gita*, New York:

Nicolas Hays, Ltd, 1976. IX-XIII.

1977

_________. "La Philosophie de la Religion devant le Pluralisme Philosophique et la Pluralité des religions." *Archivo di Filosofia: Pluralisme Philosophique et Pluralité des Religions.* 45 (Padua, cedam, 1977) pp. 193-201.

--an abridged form "Athens or Jerusalem? Philosophy or Religion." *Logos* 2 (University of Santa Clara 1981) pp. 21-39.

_________. "Social Ministry and Ministry of Word and Worship." in Achútegui, pedro de , SJ, ed., *Asian Colloquium on ministries in the Church. Hong Kong February 27- March 5, 1977* (Manila 1977) pp. 256-274.

_________. "Man as a Ritual Being." *Chicago Studies* XVI, 1 (Spring- 1977) pp. 5-28.

--Also in *Indian Theological Studies* 16 (1979) pp 6-31.

_________. "The New Innocence" *Cross Currents* XXVII (Spring 1977) pp. 7-15.

_________. "Prospettive Cristiane in Asia" (Interview). *Mondo e Missione* (Jun.-Jul., 1977) pp. 398-399.

_________. "Alternatives to Modern Culture. Provisional Draft concerning the Feasibility of a UNESCO Major Project." in *Filosofia e Disinovlvimiento. I-II Atas da III Semana internacional de Filosofia realizada na Cida de Salvador Ba de 17 a 23 Julho de 1976* (Rio de Janeiro 1977) pp. 395-398.

--Also as: "Alternatives to Modern Culture." *Interculture-77 --- (Oct.-Dec., 1982) pp. 2-4.

--"Alternatives to Modern Cultures." In *The Whole Earth Papers* (Voices from India), 1 (Winter 1978) pp. 58-61.

_________. "Creation and Nothingness. Creation: exnihilo sed non in nihilum. Nothingness: ad quem sed non a quo." *Theologiche Zeitschrift.* 33 (September- October 1977) pp. 344-352.

_________. "Colligite Fragmenta: For an Integration of Reality." in F.A. Eigo and S.E. Fittipaldi, eds., *From Alienation to At-Oneness. Proceedings of the Theology Institute of Villanova University.* Villanova:

The Villanova University Press, 1977, pp. 19-91.

_________. "The Time of Death: the Death of Time. An Indian Reflection." *La réflexion sur la mort.* [Proceedings of the II Symposion International de Philosophie]. Athens: École libre de Philosophie `Pléton', 1977, pp. 102-121.

_________. "Eine unvollendete Symphonie." in G. Neske, ed., *Erinnerung on Martin Heidegger.* Pfullingen: NESKE, 1977, pp. 173-178.

_________. "Samdhya the Vedic prayer." *Indian Theological Studies* 14 (Bangalore 1977) pp. 22-38.

1978

_________. "Religion ou Politique: Y a-t-il une solution au problème de l'Occident?." *Archivo di Filosofia I nuovi Aspetti della dimitizzazione: Religione e Politica.* 46 (Padua: cedam, 1976) pp. 73-82.

--"Non dualistic Relation between Religion and Politics." *Religion and Society* XXV (Sept., 1978) pp. 53-63.

_________. "The Bostonian Verities: A comment on the Boston Affirmations."' *Andover Newton Quarterly* XVIII, 3 (January 1978) pp. 145-153.

_________. "Man and his Spirituality." *Forum for Correspondence and Contact* 9 (Jan., 1978) pp. 58-61.

_________. "The Texture of a Text: in Response to Paul Ricoeur." *Point of Contact.* (April-May, 1978) pp. 51-64.

_________. "The Vitality and Role of Indian Philosophy Today." *Indian Philosophical Quarterly* 5 (July, 1978) pp. 673-692.

_________. "Philosophy as Life-Style." in A. Mercier and M. Svilar, eds., *Philosophers on their own Work.* Vol., IV, Berne: Peter Lang, 1978, pp. 193-228.

_________. "Time and Sacrifice. The Sacrifice of Time and the Ritual of Modernity." in J.T. Fraser, N. Lawrence and D. Park, eds., *The Study of Time III., Proceedings of the III Conference of the International Society for the Study of Time, Alpbad - Austria* (Berlin 1978) pp. 683-725.

_______. "Hermeneutics of Comparative Religion: Paradigms and Models." *The Journal of Religious Studies* VI, 1 (Spring) 1978. pp. 38-51.

--Also in *Journal of Dharma* V, 1 (Jan-Mar., 1980) pp. 38-51.

_______. "`Gedankenfreie' Meditation oder seinserfullte Gelassenheit?" In *Munen Muso~. Ungegenständliche Meditation.* [Festschrift fur Hugo M. Enomiya-Lassalle, S.J.zum 80. Geburtstag] Edited by G. Stachel. Mainz Grünewald, 1978, pp. 309-316.

_______. "The Rhetoric of interreligious dialogue p. 367-380 *Jeevadhara* 8(Kottayam 1978) pp. 367-380.

1979

_______. "*Rtatattva*: A Preface to a Hindu-Christian Theology." IX, *Jeevadhara* (Jan-Feb., 1979) pp. 6-63.

_______. "The Myth of Pluralism: The Tower of Babel - A Meditation on Non-Violence." *Cross-Currents* 29 (Summer, 1979) pp. 197-230.

_______. "Some Words instead of a Response." *Cross-Currents* 29, (Summer 1979) pp. 193-196.

_______. "Response to Harold Coward." *Cross Currents* 29 (Summer 1979) pp. 190-192.

_______. "La Religión del Futuro o la Crisis del concepto de religión: La religiosidad Humana." *Civiltà delle Macchine.* (Roma) XXVII, no., 4-6 (Lug-Dic., 1979) pp. 82-90.

_______. "Religione e Cultura: Prolegomeni." (Conversazione di Francesco d'Arcais con Raimundo Panikkar e Milan Simcic^)." *Civiltá delle Macchine.* Roma, XXVII, no., 4-6 (Lug-Dic.,) 1979, pp. 6-16.

_______. "Common Patterns of Eastern and Western Scholasticism." in *Actos del V Congreso Internacional de Filosofía Medieval.* Vol., II, Madrid: Editora Nacional, 1979, pp. 1059-1066.

_______. "Hinduism, Church and," *New Catholic Encyclopedia,* Vol., XVII *Supplement: Change in the Church.* Edited by the Catholic University of America, Washington DC & New York: Book Company, 1979, pp. 257-259.

__________. "Reflexoes Interculturais sobre a Filosofia da Linguagem." *Presença Filosófica*, V, 2. Raio da Janeiro (Abril-Junho, 1979) pp. 14-23.

__________. "You are Witnesses of This: A Symposium." Santa Cruz: Holy Trinity Monastery, 1979. A Dialogue with B. Barnhart and D. Nicholl. 45 pp.

__________. Preface to *Theresa of Avila: The Interior Castle*, trans. by Kieran Kavanaugh o.c.d and Otilio Rodriguez o.c.d., New York: Paulist Press, 1979, pp. xi-xix.

1980

__________. "Words and Terms." in *Existenza, Mito Ermeneutica (Scritti per Enrico Castelli)* Vol., II. Edited by M. Olivetti. (*Archivo di Filosofia*) Padova: CEDAM, 1980, pp. 117-133.

__________. "Some Theses on Philosophy and Liberation." *Monchanin* 13 (July - September 1980) pp. 39-40.

__________. "Chronicles." *Journal of Dharma* V (Oct-Dec., 1980) pp. 415-424.

__________. "Aporias in the Comparative Philosophy of Religion." *Man and World.* 13, 3-4 (1980) pp. 357-383.

__________. "A Philosophy of Liberation." Book Review of *Filosophia de la Liberación*, by Enrique Dussel, Mexico: Editoriar Edicol, S.A. 1977, in *Cross Currents* XXX, Winter 1980-81, pp.454-455.

__________. "Che accade all'uomo quando muore?" *Bozze*, 80 (1980) pp. 117- 136.

1981

__________. "Indian Theology: A Theological Mutation." in M. Amaladass, T.K. John, G. Gispert-Sauch, eds., *Theologizing in India. Selection of Papers presented at the Seminar held at Pune on October 26-30, 1978* (Bangalore 1981) pp. 23-42

__________. "L'eau et la Mort. Réflexion interculturelle sur une métaphore." *Archivio di Filosofia: Filosofia e Religione di fronte alla Morte.* 49 (1981) pp. 481-502.

__________. "Letter to friends of Salvador de Bahìa." *Monchanin* 70 (Jan-Mar., 1981) pp. 37-43.

________. "Man and Religion: a Dialogue with Panikkar." [A Dialogue between Panikkar and Koothottil]. *Jeevadhara* XI (Jan-Feb., 1981) pp. 5-32.

________. "Inde et Europe, Indiens et Chrétiens: Danser ensemble." (Dialogue entre R.Panikkar and G.Deleury), *Foi et Solidarité des Peuples* Document 5 [Dialogue entre R. Panikkar and G. Deleury] (Avril-1981) pp. 2-45.

________. "The Contemplative Mood: A Challenge to Modernity." *Cross-Currents* XXXI, 3 (Fall, 1981) pp. 261-272.

________. "Is History the Measure of Man? Three Kairological Moments of Human Consciousness." *The Teilhard Review.* 16, 1&2 (London, 1981) pp. 39-45.

________. "Is there Place for the *Temple* in the Modern City?" *Changing Perception of Development Problems.* Edited by R.P. Misra and M.Honjo. Nagoya, Japan: United Nations Centre for regional Development; Singapore: Maruzen Asia, 1981, pp. 275-288.

________. "Per una cultura transculturale del Simbolo." in C. Brutti, F. Scotti, eds., *Simbolo e Simbolizzazione* [Quaderni di Psicoterapia infantile 5] (Roma 1981) pp. 53-91.

________. `Rejoinds' the Reviews of *Myth, Faith and Hermeneutics*, given by S. Fttipaldi, P. Knitter, K. Mitra, J. Ramish, in *Horizons* (CTS) 8 (Spring 1981) pp. 122-131)., in *Horizons* 8 (Spring 1981) pp. 132-134.

1982

________. "Intercultural Reflections on Philosophy of Language." *Presença Filosofica.* `Filosofia e Comunicaçao~', Rìo de Janeiro, vol., III (Jan-Jun., 1982) pp. 88-92.

________. "Un futuro comune una stessa domanda per l'uomo. Tra Oriente e Occidente." *Rivivere.* Anno II (Gen.-Feb., 1982) pp. 15-20.

________. "Un Progetto di Teologia Indù-Cristiana." in *Dove va la Teologia. Il Libro Europeo* 5 (January-April 1982) pp. 113-121.

________. "Toward an ecumenical Ecumenism." *Journal of Ecumenical Studies* XIX, 4 (Fall-1982) (Editorial) pp. 781-786.

--In German: "Auf dem Wege zu einem Ökumenismus" in K. Froehlich, ed., *Ökumene. Moglichkeiten und Grenzen Heute.* [Volume in honour of Professor Oscar Cullman] Tübingen: J.C.B.Mohr, 1982, pp. 140-150.

__________. "Alternatives to Modern Culture." *Interculture* 77 (Oct.-Dec., 1982) pp. 2-4.

__________. "Alternative à la culture moderne." *Interculture* 77 Oct.-Dec., 1982) pp. 5-25.

__________. "Cross-cultural Economics." *Interculture* 77 (Oct.-Dec., 1982) pp. 26-68.

__________."Letter to Abhishiktananda: On Eastern-Western monasticism." *Studies in Formative Spirituality*. Pittsburgh (Duquesene University), III, 3 (November, 1982) pp. 427-451.

__________. "La notion de droits de l'Homme est-elle un concept occidental?" *Diogène* 120 (Paris, Gallimard, Octobre-Decembre, 1982) pp. 87-115.

--"Is the notion of Human Rights a Western Concept?" *Diogène*, no., 120 (Winter 1982) pp. 75-102.

--In Spanish: "?Es occidental el concepto de los derechos humanos?" *Diogènes* (Mexico) (Winter 1982) pp. 85-116.

__________. "El Círculo Sólo si el tiempo es circular vale la pena romperlo" in *Octavio Paz* (Madrid, Taurus), 1982, pp. 215-222.

__________. "à l'encontre de deu anthropologies." Preface to *Vers una sexologia de la Religió*, by E. Aguilar. Barcelona (Edicions 62), 1982, pp. 7-10.

__________. "Sobre l'hinduisme: i el cristianisme: Una questión de vida crisiana." *Questions de vida cristiana*. Montserrat: Publicaciones de la Abadía de Montserrat, 1982, pp. 54-72.

__________. "The Intrareligious Dialogue." *Contemporary American Theologies*, II: A Book of Readings Ed. by Deane Williams Ferm. New York: The Seabury Press, 1982, pp. 356-366.

1983

__________. "The Machine in Ancient Buddhist Prophecy." *Epiphany*, 4, (Fall, 1983) pp. 120-123.

__________. "The Global Village." *The Tablet* 9 (July, 1983) pp. 649-650.

--also "Let us stop Speaking about `the Global Village'." *Interculture* 16 (Oct-Dec., 1983) pp. 34-36.

__________. "The End of History: The Threefold Structure of Human Time-Consciousness." *Teilhard and the unity of Knowledge.* Edited by Thomas M. King and James F. Salamon. New York: Paulist Press, 1983, pp. 83-141.

--Italian "La fine della storia: la triplice struttura della conscienza umana del tempo." *Quaderni di psicoterapia infantile: Tempo e Psicoanalisi.* Perugia, Borla, 1984, pp. 16-109.

__________. "La vocation humaine est fondamentalement religieuse? Recontre avec R. Panikkar." *Nouveau Dialogue* (SIF), no., 51 (Sept., 1983) pp. 3 - 11.

__________. "Interview." [R.Panikkar interviewed by Peter Reinhart]. *Epiphany* 3 (Summer, 1983) pp. 2-31.

__________. "Prefazione." *Liberaci dal male. Male e vie di liberazione nelle Religioni.* Bologna: La Nuova Stampa, 1983, pp. 7-19.

__________. "Regard sur l'Avenir de la Mission." *Bulletin de l'entraide Missionnaire* 25 (September 1983) pp. 137-147.

1984

__________. "The Cosmotheandric Intuition." *Jeevadhara* -79 (Jan. 1984) pp. 27-35.

__________. "L'atteggiamento contemplativo: una sfida per la modernitá" in *Contemplazione e ricerca spirituale nella societá se colarizzata. La proposta di Merton e Maritaian.* Milano: Massimo, 1984, pp. 37-52.

__________. "Religione e filosofie dell'Oriente." *Nouva Secondaria -* 8. Brecia (La Scuola), April, 1984, p. 41.

__________. "A Dialogue on Human Rights." *Interculture - 83* (April-June, 1984) pp. 78-82.

__________. "Response Regarding Media, Electioneering and Human Values." *Forum* 14 (June, 1984) pp. 46-47.

__________. "The Dialogical Dialogue". In *The World's Religious Traditions: Current Perspectives in Religious Studies. Essays in Honour of Wilfred Cantwell Smith.* Edited by Frank Whaling. Edinburgh: T. &

T. Clark., 1984, pp. 61-72.

__________. "La pau política com a objectiù religiós." *Questions de Vida Cristiana*. 121, Montserrat: Publicacions de l'Abadia de Montserrat, 1984, pp. 83-84.

__________. "La Interpellaciò del'Asia al Cristianisme." *Theologia i Vida*.Barcelona: Editorial Claret, 1984, pp. 81-93.

__________. "Quelques thèses supplémentaires sur la technologie". In *Philosophie et technique*, edited by André Mercier. Berne and Paris: Institut International de Philosophie, 1984, pp. 61-72.

__________. "Religious Pluralism: The Metaphysical Challenge". In *Religious Pluralism*. Notre Dame: Notre Dame University Press, 1984, pp. 97-115.

__________. "Sein und Nichts: Fragender Durchblick auf die entfaltete Problematik". In *Sein und Nichts in der Abendländischen Mystik*, edited by Walter Strolz. Freiburg, Basel, Wien: Herder, 1984, pp. 107-123.

__________. "L'émancipation de la théologie". In *Interculture* 85 (Octobre-Decembre 1984) pp. 22-37.

__________. "The Dream of an Indian Ecclesiology". In *Searching for an Indian Ecclesiology*, edited by Indian Theological Association, Bangalore: Asian Trading Corporation, 1984, pp. 24-54.

__________. "The Destiny of Technological Civilization: An Ancient Buddhist Legend: Romavisaya". In *Alternatives. A Journal of World Policy*. X (Fall, 1984) pp. 237 -253.

__________. "The Catholic Experience Towards a Theoanthropocosmic Vision". In *Was ist die Natur*, Edited by the Institut für Interkulturelle Forschung in Japan, Kyoto. Japan: Verlag Hozokan, 1984, pp. 83 -107.

__________. "La grazia di Babele". In *Bozze* 84 (1984) Rome.

1985

__________. "Religion and Politics: The Western Dilemma". In *Religion and Politics in the Modern World*, edited by Peter H. Merkl and Ninian Smart, New York and London: New York University Press, 1985, pp. 44-90.

________. "Una perspectiva intercultural de la `teología de la liberación'" In *El Pais* Madrid (February 11, 1985) pp. 9-10.

________. "Global Perspectives: Spiritualities in Interaction." *Journal of Dharma* 10 (January- March 1985) pp. 6-17.

________. "Foreword". In *Heat and Sacrifice in the Vedas*, by UMā-Marina Vesci. Delhi, Varanasi, Patna, Madras: Motilal Banarsidass, 1985, pp. xi -xvii.

________. "Der Mensch, ein trinitarisches Mysterium". In *Die Verantwortung des Menschen für eine bewohnbere Welt im Christentum, Hinduismus und Buddhismus.* Edited by R. Panikkar and W. Strolz, Freiburg: Herder, 1985, pp. 147 -150.

________. "Dios en las Religiones". In *Misión Abierta.*[Special volume dedicated to the V Congress of Theology: Madrid-Septiembre -1985]. Madrid (1985) Nrs.5-6, pp. 85 - 102.

________. "Présentation. Un traité de spiritualité." Préface to *La voie Jaina: histoire, spiritualité, vie des ascètes pèlerins de l'Inde*, by N. Shanta. Paris: O.E.I.L. --Collection les deux rives-- 1985, pp. 17-32.

________. "Qué vol dir avui confessar-se cristiá?". In *Questions de vida cristiana*, Nr. 128 - 129. Montserrat: Publications de l'Abadia de Montserrat, 1985, pp. 86-111.

________. "Foreword." to *The Vision of Cosmic Order in the Vedas*, by Jeanine Miller. London: Routledge & Kegan Paul, 1985, pp.xi- xix.

________. "Present-Day University Education and World Cultures". In *Interculture*, (Summer 1985) pp. 2-15.

________. "Cultural Disarmament." [Foreword to the Summary of a research conducted by R. Rapp under the guidance of R. Panikkar in UCSB - 1984]. In *Interculture*, (Fall, 1985) p. 14.

________. "The Sermon on the mount of intrareligious Dialogue." (Editorial) in *Journal of Ecumenical Studies* XXII (Fall, 1985) p. 773.

1986

________. "Some Thesis on Technology". In *Logos* 7 (1986) pp. 115-124.

________. "La Montée vers le Fond." Préface a H. Le Saux (Abhishitananda) *La Montée Au Fond Du Coeur Le journal intime du moine chrétien-sannyāsi hindou*. Paris: O.E.I.L., Les Deux Rives.

________. "The Jesus Debate. Cross-Cultural Considerations". [Review of *The Jesus Debate* by William Thompson] In *The Ecumenist*, 24, (Jul-Aug., 1986) pp. 72-76.

________. "Un Tirano Anonimo" i "La Torre di Babele." *L'Altrapagina*, no., 6 (Giugno 1986) p. 6.

________. "The Threefold Linguistic Intrasubjectivity." *Archivio Di Filosofia* LIV, no., 1-3 (1986) pp. 593-606.

________. "The Pope and the Angels." *The Tablet* 240, no., 7632 (Oct., 1986) p. 1098.

________. "Medicina y Religión." *Jano*, no., 737 (Jul., 1986) pp. 12-48.

________. "La dialéctica de la razón armada." (Entrevista) *Concordia*, 9 (1986), pp. 68-89.

1987

________. "The Challenge of Religious Studies to the Issues of our Times". Foreword to Scott Eastham, *Nucleus: Reconnecting Science and Religion in the Nuclear Age*. Beard and Co., 1987, pp. xiii-xxxviii.

________. "Letter to a Young Monk". *Living Prayer* (Nov.-Dec., 1987) pp.11-14.

________. "El Somni d'una Església India." *Questions de Vida Cristiana* 131-132 (Montserrat 1987) pp. 174-199.

________. "Els dimonis de Joan Paul II." *Questions de Vida Cristiana*, no., 135-136 (Montserrat 1987) pp. 142-143.

________. "Una critica inter - cultural de la Teologia de l'alliberament." *Questions de Vida Cristiana*, no., 135-136, (Montserrat 1987) pp. 144-146.

________. "Prof. Raimundo Panikkar" [Abbreviation of the talk given by Panikkar in Dharmaram, Bangalore]. *Dharmaram Vidya Kshetram Newsletter* 2, no. 1 (Sept., 1987) pp. 19.

________. "Indic theological series: an introduction." *Indian Theological Studies* 24 (1987) pp. 252-261. Also in *Indian Missiological Review* 9 (1987) pp. 336-334; in *Jeevadhara* 17 (1987) pp. 416-422; in *Word and Woship* 20 (1987) pp. 331-338.

B. *Secondary Sources*: *The Literature Referring to Panikkar*

1. Books and Articles

BAHR, ANN MARIE. "Ecumenical Events." [Summary of the Conference `Toward a Universal Theology of Religion' held at Temple University, October 17-19, 1984] *Journal of Ecumenical Studies* 22 (Winter 1984) pp. 194-198.

BALWANT, PARADKAR. "The Christian Encounter with men of other faiths." *Religion and Society*, XIV, no., 2.

BIELAWSKI, MACIEJ. "Panikkar: His Life and His Works," Campo Dei Fiori, 2018.

CAPPS, WALTER H., "Toward a Christian theology of the World's Religions." *Cross Currents* 29 (Summer 1979) pp. 156-168, 182.

CHAUMEIL M.J., "Madame Daniélou en son temps." *Cahiers de Neuilly* (January, 1967) pp. 5-63.

CHETHIMATTAM, J.B. CMI. "Indian Approaches to Christology: R. Panikker's approach to Christology." *The Indian Journal of Theology* 23 (1974) pp. 219-222.

CLEMENT OLIVIER, "Rencontre." *Axes* 7 (1974-1975) pp. 167-172.

CRACKNELL, KENNETH. "Christianity and Religious Pluralism: The Ethics of Interfaith relations. *Christian Jewish Relations*, 18, no., 2 (June, 1985) pp. 40-58.

COUSINS, EWERT H., "Introduction: The Panikkar Symposium at Santa Barbara." *Cross Currents* 29 (Summer 1979) pp. 131-134, 140.

COUSINS, EWERT H., "Raimundo Panikkar and the Christian systematic theology of the future." *Cross Currents* 29 (Summer 1979) pp. 141-155.

COWARD, HAROLD G., "Panikker's Approach to Interreligious Dialogue." *Cross Currents* 29 (Summer 1979) pp. 183-189. 192.

CULLMANN OSCAR, "Rencontre." *Axes* 7 (1974-1975) pp. 173-175.

DANKFRIED, REETZ. "Raymond Panikkar's theology of religions." *Religion and Society* XV, no., 3 (1968) pp. 46-54.

D'COSTA, GAVIN. "Karl Rahner's anonymous Christian: a reappraisal." *Modern Theology* 1 (January 1985) pp. 131-148.

DE GANDILLAC, MAURICE. "Jean Daniélou et'Dieu Vivant'." *Axes* 7 (1974 - 1975) pp. 125-130.

DEVADAS, NALINI. "The Theandrism of Raimundo Panikkar and Trinitarian Parallels in Modern Hindu Thought." *Journal of Ecumenical Studies* 17 (1980) pp. 606-620.

D'SA, FRANCIS. "Myth, History and Cosmos." *Jeevadhara* XIV, no., 79 (1984) pp. 7-26.

D'Sa, Francis X. "Panikkar, Raimon (1918-2010)." ACPI *Encyclopedia of Philosophy.* Ed. Johnson J. Puthenpurackal. Bangalore: ATC 2010.

D'SOUZA, JEROME, S.J. "Exploding the Myth of East and West." *Worldmission* 9, no., 1 (1958) pp. 23-32.

DUPUIS, J. "The presence of Christ in Hinduism." *Clergy Monthly,* 34, pp.141-148.

__________. "Trinity and World Religions: Some Reflections on a Recent Book." *Clergy Monthly,* 35 (Feb., 1971) pp. 77-80.

__________. *Jesus Christ and His Spirit.* Bangalore: Theological Publications in India, 1977.

EMPRAYIL, THOMAS, V.C. *The Emerging Theology of Religions: The Contribution of the Catholic Church in India.* India: Vincentian Publications, 1980.

FRIES, HEINRICH. "Heil im Hinduismus." *In Heil in den Religionen und im Christentum,* Heinrich Fries; J. Brosseder; H. Bürkle; F. Köster; and F. Wolfinger. St. Ottilien: Eos Verlag Erzabtei, 1982, pp. 30-53.

GISPERT-SAUCH, G. "Raimon Panikkar." *Vidyajyoti: Journal of Theological Reflection,* December 2010.

GOMES, FELIPE, sj. "The Uniqueness and Universality of Christ." *East Asian Pastoral Review* XX, no., 1 (1983) pp. 4-30.

GOULET, JACQUES. "The Ultimate Indiscernibility of Faith." *African Ecclesial Review* 22 (Oct. 1980) pp. 288-293.

GRIFFITHS, BEDE. *Christ in India: Essays Towards a Hindu Christian Dialogue.* Bangalore: Asian Trading Corporation, 1986.

HARDON, JOHN A. *Gott in den Religionen der Welt*, München: Rex-Verlag Luzern, 1967.

HERBSTRITH, WALTRAUD. *Begegnung mit Indien: und einem seiner gro$en christlichen Pioniere Kuriackos Elias Chavara*. Trier: Johann Josef Zimmer Verlag, 1969.

JOSEP-IGNASI Saranyan Raimon Panikkar: a propósito de una biografía (in: *Studia et Documenta* 2017, Vol. 11, p. 323-348).

KAROKARAN, ANTO. *Evangelization and diakonia: A Study in the Evangelization and diakonia: A Study in the Indian Perspective.* Dharmaram Publications, Bangalore 1978 pp. 140-158; 206-211.

KNITTER, PAUL F. "Theocentric Christology", *Theology Today* 40 (July 1983) pp. 130-149.

__________. *No Other Name? A Critical Survey of Christian Attitudes toward the World Religions.* London: SCM Press, 1985, pp. 145-167.

KOMULAINEN. JYRI *An Emerging Cosmotheandric Religion?: Raimon Panikkar's Pluralistic Theology Of Religions* .Boston: Brill Academic Publishers, 2005.

KOOTHOTIL, ABRAHAM. "Man and Religion: A Dialogue with Panikkar." *Jeevadhara* 11 (1981) pp. 5-43.

KÜNG, HANS. *Theologie im Aufbruch*. München: Piper 1987.

LUKE, K. "Mythical Language, its Origin and Significance." *Jeevadhara* XIV, no., 79 (1984) pp. 36-51.

MACQUARRIE, JOHN. "Some Problems of Modern Christology" *Jeevadhara*. 23 (1974) pp. 155-175.

MENACHERRY, CHERIYAN. *Christ: The Mystery in History: A Critical Study on the Christology of Raymond Panikkar.* Peter Lang Publ Inc. (June 1996)

__________. *Confluence of Religions, Panikkar's Christological prayāṇa 1*, Chisinau, Moldova: Blessed Hope Publishing, 2022, pp. 34-35.

__________. *Einmündung der Religionen: Panikkars christologisches prayāṇa 1*, Chisinau, Moldova: Fromm Verlag, 2022.

MILLER, JEANINE. *The Vision of Cosmic Order in the Vedas.* Foreword by Raimundo Panikkar. London: Routledge & Kegan Paul, 1985.

MITRA KANA, *Catholicism and Hinduism. A Vedantic Investigation of Raimundo Panikkar's Attempt at Bridge Building* (Unpublished doctoral thesis) (Temple University 1980).

MOLINARIO F., "L'evangelizzazione delle Culture e delle Religioni nella Esperienza e negli Scritti di Raymond Panikkar." *Testimonianza* 15 (1977) pp. 314-341.

MOOKENTHOTTAM, ANTONY M.S.F.S. *Indian Theological Tendencies: Approaches and Problems for Further Research as Seen in the Works of Some Leading Indian Theologians.* Frankfurt: Peter Lang, 1978.

________. *Towards a Theology in the Indian Context.* Bangalore: Asian Trading Corporation, 1980.

MORETA, IGNASI. "Raimon Panikkar: an intense life, intercultural thought," in Barcelona Metropolis,

https://www.barcelona.cat/bcnmetropolis/2007-2017/en/calaixera/biografies/raimon-panikkar-una-vida-intensa-un-pensament-intercultural/#:~:text=Panikkar%20was%20born%20in%20Barcelona,Germany%2C%20where%20he%20studied%20chemistry

MULDER, D.C., "Rymond Panikkar's Dialog Met Het Hindoeìsme'." *Gereformeers Theologisch Tiydschrift* (August, 1969) pp. 186-198.

MUNDADAN, A.M. "Hindu-Christian Dialogue: Past Twenty Five Years." (A Survey of Indian Christian Literature) *Jeevadhara*, XI (1981) pp. 375-394.

NÉDONCELLE, MAURICE. "Philosophie de la Religion." in *La Philosophie Contemporaine.* Edited by Raymond Klibansky. Firenz: La Nuova Italia Editrice 1971, pp. 170-213.

NELSON, BENJAMIN. "A New Science of Civilizational analysis: A Tribute to Panikkar." *Cross Currents* 29 (Summer 1979) pp. 135-140.

NEUMAN MARTIN, "New Approaches for Benedictine Studies: A Review Essay of Raimundo Panikkar's *Blessed Simplicity.*" *The American Benedictine Review* 35 (June 1984) pp. 128-145.

PANDIKATTU, KURUVILLA Christian Advaita as the Hermeneutic Key to Bede Griffiths' Understanding of Inter-religious Dialogue. Ph D Thesis in Theology, Innsbruck: Univ of Innsbruck, 1996. (Chapter 2 on Panikkar)

PANIKKAR, R., Curriculum Vitae. "List of Books and Selected Articles." Santa Barbara 1984.

PANUNZIO, S., "Christus und Indian. Jesus und Wir." (Eigespräch in Rom über 'Māyā e Apocalisse' von Raimundo Panikkar) Interventions by Panunzio, Sforza, Vereno, Trevisonno, Fortunato and Panikkar, *Kairos* (1968) pp. 115-132.

PARAPPALLY, JACOB *Emerging Trends in Indian Christology: A Critical Study of the Development, Context and Contemporary Catholic Attempts of R.Panikkar and S.Kappen to Articulate a Relevant Christology in Indian Context.* (1992) by, MSFS,

PARRINDER, GEOFFREY. *Avatar and Incarnation.* New York: Oxford University Press, 1982.

OHM, THOMAS. *Asiens Nein und Ja zum westlichen Christentum.* Zweit, neu bearbeitet Auflage. Münhen: Kösel- Verlag, 1960.

__________. "Geben Sie uns ein Christusbuch." *Der Chrisliche Sonntag*, XIII, no., 39 (1961).

PIRYNS, ERNEST D. "Current Roman Catholic Views of other Religions." *Missionalia* 13 (August 1985) pp. 55-62.

PODGORSKI, FRANK. "Contemplatio: The Cosmotheandric insight of Raimundo Panikkar." *Logos* 2, 1981, pp. 41-57.

RAJ, ANTHONY SAVARI. *A New Hermeneutic of Reality: Raimon Panikkar's Cosmotheandric Vision.* Peter Lang Publishing (August 1998)

"RAYMOND PANIKKAR (Close-up)." *Jubilee* 13 (Oct. 1965) pp. 24-25.

REETZ, D. "Raymond Panikkar's Theology of Religions." *Religion and Society* 15, no.,3 (1968) pp. 32-55.

ROBINSON, JOHN A.T. *Truth is Two-Eyed*, London: SCM Press, 1979.

SALDANHA, CHRYS. *Divine Pedagogy. A Patristic View of Non-Christian Religions* (Biblioteca di Scienze Religiose 57. Rome 1984.

SALTER, PETER. "Three Types of Reasoning in Religion", *Journal of American Academy of Religion* 49, no., 1 (1982) pp. 17-34.

__________. "Hindu and Christian Symbols in the work of R. Panikkar." *Cross Currents* 29 (1979) pp. 169-182.

SMET, ROBERT. *Essai sur la pensée de Raimundo Panikkar, une contribution indienne à la théologie des religions et à la Christologie.* Louvain-la-Neuve: Centre d'Histoire des Religions, 1981.

__________. *Le Problème d'une théologie Hindoue-Chrétienne selon Raymond Panikkar.* Louvain-La-Neuve: Centre d'Histoire des Religions, 1983.

VALLUVASSERY, CLEMENT. *Christus im Kontext und Kontext in Christus: Chalcedon und indische Christologie bei Raimon Panikkar und Samuel Rayan.* Münster: LIT Verlag. 2001.

VATTAKERIL, PETER. *Dialogue with men of other faiths: its theological implications. A critical study of Raimundo Panikkar.* (Excerpta ex dissertation ad Doctoratum in Facultatae Theologiae Pontificiae Universitatis Gregorianae). Roma: Pontificia Universitas Gregorianum, 1986.

VELIATH, DOMINIC. *Understanding of Religions: Jean Daniélou and Raimundo Panikkar, A Study in Contrast.* Bangalore: Kristujoyti College, 1981.

2. Book Reviews

ARGAUD, JACKY. Review of *Le Dialogue Intrareligieux,* by Panikkar, in *Etudes Theologiques et Religieuses,* 61, no., 3 (1986) pp. 468-469.

BARNES, M. Review of *Myth, Faith and Hermeneutics,* by Panikkar, in *Month,* 10 (Summer 1977) p. 319.

BHATTACHARYA, C. Review of *The Intra-Religious Dialogue,* by Panikkar, in *Religious Education* 74 (Nov-Dec., 1979) pp. 679-680.

BONNICHON, A. *Review of Lettre sur l'Inde,* by Panikkar, in *Etudes,* 320 (March 1964) p. 416.

BRENNAN, E. Review of *Myth, Faith and Hermeneutics,* by Panikkar, in *Journal of Ecumenical Studies,* 18 (Summer 1981) pp. 505-506.

CAMPBELL, T. Review of *The Intra-Religious Dialogue*, by Panikkar, in *Sisters Today*, 50 (April 1979) p. 590.

CHARLES, JOHN. Bro. Review of *Blessed Simplicity: The Monk as Universal Archetype*, by Panikkar, in *Spiritual Life*, 29 (Summer 1983) p. 115.

CHETHIMATTAM, J. Review of *The Vedic Experience: Mantramanjari*, by R. Panikkar, in *Thought*, 54 (Dec., 1979) p. 432.

CORBISHLEY, T. Review of *Worship and Secular Man*, by Panikkar, in *Month* 6 (July, 1973) p. 250.

COWARD, HAROLD. Review of *Myth, Faith and Hermeneutics*, by Panikkar, in *Journal of American Academy of Religion*, 49 (Dec., 1981) pp. 728-729.

__________. Review of *The Unknown Christ of Hinduism: Towards An Ecumenical Christophany*, by Panikkar, in *Religious Studies Bulletin*, 4 (Jan. 1984) pp. 33-35

CRACKNELL, K. Review of *Myth, Faith and Hermeneutics*, by Panikkar, in *Theology*, 85 (March 1982) pp. 144-145.

DEADY, E. Review of *Worship and Secular Man*, by Panikkar, in *Living Light*, 11 (Summer 1974) pp. 319-320.

DE LETTER, P. Review of *Kultmysterium in Hinduismus und Christentum: Ein Beitrag zur vergleichenden Religionstheololgie*, by Panikkar, in *The Clergy Monthly* (Supplement to) XXIX (Sept., 1965) pp. 301-302.

--Also in *Theologische Revue*, nr. 6 (1967) pp. 370-378.

DE NICHOLÅS, A. Review of *Blessed Simplicity: The Monk as Universal Archetype*, by Panikkar, in *Cross Currents*, 32 (Winter 1982-1983) pp. 470-473.

DEVINE, G. Review of *Worship and Secular Man*, by Panikkar, in *Cross Currents*, 23 (Summer 1973) pp. 211-212.

DHAVAMONY, M. Review of *The Unknown Christ of Hinduism*, by R. Panikkar, in *The Heythrop Journal*, 6 (Oct., 1986) pp. 479-481.

DUPUIS, J., Review of *The Unknown Christ of Hinduism*, by R. Panikkar, in *The Clergy Monthly* (Supplement to) XXIX (Sept., 1965) pp. 278-283.

__________. "Trinity and World Religions: Some Reflections on a Recent Book." *Clergy Monthly*, 35 (Feb., 1971) pp. 77-80.

__________. Review of *The Intra-Religious Dialogue*, by Panikkar, in *Vidyajyoti* (December 1979) p. 537.

__________. Review of *The Unknown Christ of Hinduism: Towards an Ecumenical Christophany*, by R. Panikkar, in Vidyajyoti (May-June 1982) pp. 256-257.

EARLING, B. Review of *Myth, Faith and Hermeneutics*, by Panikkar, in *Dialogue*, 21 (Winter 1982) pp. 67-68.

ÉTIENNE, J. Review of *Le Culte et l'homme Séculier*, by Panikkar, in *Revue Theologique Louvain*, 8, no., 1, p. 87.

FARRELLY, M. Review of *The Trinity and the Religious Experience of Man*, by Panikkar, in *American Ecclesiastical Reviews*, 168 (Oct., 1974) pp. 568-569.

FISKE, A. Review of *The Vedic Experience: Mantramanjari*, by Panikkar, in *Cross Currents*, 27 (Fall, 1977) p. 337.

FITTIPALDI, S. Review of *Myth, Faith and Hermeneutics*, by Panikkar, in *Horizons* (CTS) 8 (Spring 1981) 122-125.

--Also Panikkar (Rejoinder) in *Horizons*, 8 (Spring 1981) pp. 132-134

Review of *The Unknown Christ of Hinduism: Towards An Ecumenical Christophany*, by Panikkar, in *Journal of Ecumenical Studies*, 19 (Fall 1982) pp. 827-828.

FORD, J. Review of *El Silencio del Dios*, by Panikkar, in *Journal of Ecumenical Studies*, 9 (Summer 1972) p. 614.

FRISON, P. Review of *Le Christ et l'hindouisme*, by Panikkar, in *Etudes* 337 (Oct. 1972) p. 480.

HANUS, J. Review of *Blessed Simplicity: The Monk as Universal Archetype*, by Panikkar, in *Spirituality Today*, 35 (Summer 1983) p. 186.

HEALY, K. Sr. Review of *Blessed Simplicity: The Monk as Universal Archetype*, by Panikkar, in *Review for Religious*, 42 (Sept-Oct. 1983) p. 790.

HOCKEN, P. Review of *Worship and Secular Man*, by Panikkar, in *Clergy Review*, 59 (Dec. 1974) pp. 839-841.

HOLSTEIN, H. Review of *Le Mystère du Culte dans l'Hindouisme et le Christianisme*, by Panikkar, in *Etudes*, 335 (Oct. 1971) p. 476.

HOPKINS, S. Review of *The Unknown Christ of Hinduism: Towards an Ecumenical Christophany*, by Panikkar, in *Cross Currents* 31 (Summer 1981) Pp. 214-216.

HOOKER, R H. Review of *The Unknown Christ of Hinduism: Towards An Ecumenical Christophany*, by Panikkar, in *International Bulletin of Missionary Research*, 7 (April 1983) p. 80.

KAUFMAN, P L. Review of *Myth, Faith and Hermeneutics*, by Panikkar, in *Journal of Psychology and Theology*, 10 (Sum. 1982) p. 183.

KING, U. Review of *The Vedic Experience: Mantramanjari*, by Panikkar, in *Teilhard Review*, 13 (Winter 1978) p. 138.

KITAGAWA, J M. Review of *Myth, Faith and Hermeneutics*, by Panikkar, in *Anglican Theological Review*, 64 (April 1982) pp. 254-258.

KNITTER, P.F. Review of *The Intra-Religious Dialogue*, by Panikkar, in *Horizons* (CTS), 7 (Spring 1980) pp. 152-153.

KNITTER, P. Review of *Myth, Faith and Hermeneutics*, by Panikkar, in *Horizons* (CTS) 8 (Spring 1981) 126-127.

-Also Panikkar (Rejoinder) in *Horizons*, 8 (Spring 1981) pp. 132-134.

LANE, R. Review of *Blessed Simplicity: The Monk as Universal Archetype*, by Panikkar, in *Sisters Today*, 54 (January 1983) p. 309.

LANGLEY, M S. Review of *The Unknown Christ of Hinduism: Towards An Ecumenical Christophany*, by Panikkar, in *Churchman: a Quarterly Journal of Anglican Theology*, 95, no., 4 (1981) pp. 367-368.

LEEMING, B. REVIEW of *The Unknown Christ of Hinduism*, by Panikkar, in *Clergy Review*, 52 (Sep., 1967) pp. 737-739.

MASCALL, E. Review of *The Trinity and the Religious Experience of Man: Icon - Person - Mystery*, by Panikkar, in *Month*, 7 (April 1974) pp. 554-555.

MASSON, J. Review of *The Unknown Christ of Hinduism*, by Panikkar, in *Nouvelle Revue Theologique*, 98 (Dec. 1966) p. 116.

MASSON, J. Review of *Le Mystère du Culte dans l'Hindouisme et le Christianisme*, by Panikkar, in *Nouvelle Revue Theologique*, 93 (Aug-Sep., 1971) p. 731.

McDERMOTT, R. Review of *The Unknown Christ of Hinduism*, by Panikkar, in *Cross Currents*, 16 (Spring 1966) pp. 243-245.

MITRA, K. Review of *The Trinity and the Religious Experience of Man*, by Panikkar, in *Journal of Ecumenical Studies*, 12 (Spring 1975) pp. 274-275.

MITRA, K. Review of *The Intra-Religious Dialogue*, by Panikkar, in *Journal of Ecumenical Studies*, 16 (Fall 1979) p. 768.

MITRA, K., Review of *Myth, Faith and Hermeneutics*, by Panikkar, in *Horizons* (CTS), 8 (Spring 1981) pp. 127-129.

--Also Panikkar R. (Rejoinder) in *Horizons*, 8 (Spring 1981) pp. 132-134.

NOSSENT, G. Review of *Le Culte et l'homme Séculier*, by Panikkar, in *Nouvelle Revue Theologique*, 98 (Sep-Oct. 1976) p. 762.

O'CONNOR, M. Sr. Review of *The Trinity and the Religious Experience of Man*, by Panikkar, in *Sisters Today*, 46 (June-July 1975) p. 612.

PADOUX, A. Review of *The Unknown Christ of Hinduism: Towards An Ecumenical Christophany*, by Panikkar, in *Archives de Sciences Sociales de Religions*, 28 (April-June 1983) pp. 263-264.

PENNINGTON, M. Review of *The Trinity and the Religious Experience of Man*, by Panikkar, in *Review for Religious*, 33 (Summer 1974) p. 1215.

PODGORSKI, F. Review of The Intra-Religious Dialogue, by Panikkar, in *Cross Currents*, 29 (Summer 1979) pp. 231-232.

PODGORSKI, F. Review of The Intra-Religious Dialogue, by Panikkar, in *Theological Studies*, 40 (Dec., 1979) p. 798

PODGORSKI, F. Review of *Myth, Faith and Hermeneutics*, by Panikkar, in *Cross Currents* 29 (Summer 1979) pp. 231-236.

RAMISCH, J. Review of *Myth, Faith and Hermeneutics*, by Panikkar, in *Horizons* (CTS), 8 (Spring 1981) pp. 129-131.

--Also Panikkar (Rejoinder) in *Horizons*, 8 (Spring 1981) pp. 132-134.

REINHART, P. Review of *Blessed Simplicity: The Monk as Universal Archetype*, by Panikkar, in *Epiphany*, 4 (Winter 1983) pp. 110-113.

REISER, W. Review of *The Unknown Christ of Hinduism: Towards an Ecumenical Christophany*, by Panikkar, in *Heythrop*, 23 (October 1982) p. 451.

RÉTIF, A. Review of Lettre sur l'Inde, by Panikkar, in *World Justice*, 6 (Dec. 1964) p. 221.

REVIEW of *The Unknown Christ of Hinduism*, by Panikkar, in *The Irish Ecclesiastical Record*, 104 (Aug-Sep. 1965) pp. 181-182.

REVIEW of *The Unknown Christ of Hinduism: Towards an Ecumenical Christophany*, by Panikkar, in *Bibliografia Missionaria* XLVI (1982) p. 294.

REVIEW of *The Unknown Christ of Hinduism: Towards an Ecumenical Christophany*, by Panikkar, in *Social Justice*, 73 (Sept-Oct., 1982) p. 159.

REVIEW of *Lettre sur l'Inde*, by Panikkar, in *Cristian World*, 8 (1963) p. 538.

REVIEW of *Lettre sur l'Inde*, by Panikkar, in *Lumen*, 19 (Sep. 1964) p. 592.

REVIEW of *Kultmysterium in Hinduismus und Christentum: Ein Beitrag zur vergleichenden Religionstheologie.* by Panikkar, in *Bibliographia Missionaria* XXXVII (1973), p. 172.

REVIEW of *The Trinity and the Religious Experience of Man*, by Panikkar, in *Heythrop Journal*, 16 (Jan. 1975) p. 114.

REVIEW of *The Vedic Experience. Mantraman~jarí: An Anthology of the Vedas for Modern Man and Contemporary Celebration*, by Panikkar, in *The Indian Journal of Theology* 27 (1978) pp. 89-101.

RICHARDS, M. Review of *The Trinity and the Religious Experience of Man*, by Panikkar, in *Tablet*, 228 (August 31, 1974) p. 842.

ROGERS, A M S. Review of *The Unknown Christ of Hinduism: Towards An Ecumenical Christophany*, by Panikkar, in *Ching Feng: Quarterly Notes on Christianity and Chinese Religions and Culture* (English Ed.), 26, no., 1 (April 1983) pp. 63-64.

SALIBA, J. Review of *Myth, Faith and Hermeneutics*, by Panikkar, in *Horizons* (CTS), 4 (Fall 1977) p. 285.

--Also in Theological Studies, 41 (Dec. 1980) p. 810.

SAMARTHA, S J. Review of *The Unknown Christ of Hinduism: Towards An Ecumenical Christophany*, by Panikkar, in *Religion and Society*, 30 (Mar. 1983) p. 52-61.

SCHEEN, F. Review of *The Unknown Christ of Hinduism*, by Panikkar, in *World Mission*, 16 (Summer 1965) pp. 102-104.

SEASOLTZ, K. Review of *Worship and Secular Man*, by Panikkar, in *The Jurist*, 34 (Winter-Spring 1974) pp. 230-232.

SMITH, M. Review of *The Vedic Experience: Mantramanjari*, by Panikkar, in *Journal of Ecumenical Studies*, 16 (Spring 1979) pp. 344-346.

SMITH, W C. Review of *The Intra-Religious Dialogue*, by Panikkar, in *International Bulletin of Missionary Research*, 5 (April 1981) pp. 89-90.

TUGWELL, S. Review of *Le Mystère du Culte dans l'Hindouisme et le Christianisme*, by Panikkar, in *New Blackfriars*, 53 (May 1972) pp. 237-238.

TUGWELL, S. Review of *The Vedic Experience: Mantramanjari*, by Panikkar, in *New Blackfriars*, 59 (Dec. 1978) p. 573.

TURCHETTO, G. Review of *Myth, Faith and Hermeneutics*, by Panikkar, in *Cross Currents*, 30 (Fall 1980) p. 290.

TWOMEY, J. Review of *Worship and Secular Man*, by Panikkar, in *The Furrow*, 24 (Aug. 1973) pp. 518-519.

TWOMEY, J. Review of *The Trinity and the Religious Experience of Man*, by Panikkar, in *The Furrow*, 25 (Nov. 1974) p. 633-634.

VALLÉE, G. Review of *Le Mystère du Culte dans l'Hindouisme et le Christianisme*, by Panikkar, in *Theological Studies*, 34 (March 1973) p. 184.

VETTER, TILMANN. "Weltgespräch der Relilgionen. Eine Rezension." Review of *Die Verantwortung des Menschen für eine bewohnbare Welt im Christentum, Hinduismus und Buddhismus*, by Panikkar and Walter Strolz, in *Zeitschrift für Missionswissenschaft und Religions Wissenschaft* 7 (Münster 1987) pp. 137-140.

WHITE, J. Review of *Worship and Secular Man*, by Panikkar, in *Worship*, 47 (Jun-Jul. 1973) p. 376.

WICKER, B. Review of *Worship and Secular Man*, by Panikkar, in *Tablet*, 227 (April 1973) p. 339.

WILLIAMS, M. Review of *Myth, Faith and Hermeneutics*, by Panikkar, in *Clergy Review*, 66 (Summer 81) p. 337.

WOLANIN A. Review of *The Unknown Christ of Hinduism: Towards an Ecumenical Christophany*, by Panikkar, in *Gregorianum*, 65, no., 3-2 (1984) p. 539.

ZAGO, M. Review of *Le Mystère du Culte dans l'Hindouisme et le Christianisme*, by Panikkar, in *Revue de l'universite d'Ottawa*, 43 (Jan-Mar. 1973) p. 166.

C. *Other Sources: Books and Articles Consulted*

ABBA, R. "Name," in *The Interpreter's Dictionary of the Bible*, Vol., 3, edited by George Arthur Buttrick. Nashville (USA): Abingdon Press (1962) 1982, pp. 500-508.

ABÉCASSIS, ARMAND. "Le Midrach entre le Mythos et le Logos." *Les Etudes Philosophiques* (April-June 1984) pp. 189-204.

AIYANGAR NARAYAN, *Ancient Hindu Mythology*. New Delhi: Deep & Deep Publications, 1983.

ALFARO, JUAN. "II. Faith." in K. Rahner, ed. *Encyclopedia of Theology: A Concise Sacramentum Mundi*. London: Burns & Oates, (1975) 1981. pp. 500-510.

AMALADOSS, A. "Symbol and Mystery." *Journal of Dharma* 2 (October 1977): pp. 382-396.

AMALORPAVADASS. Ed., *Research Seminar on Non-Biblical Scriptures*, Bangalore: NBCLC, 1975.

ANDERSON, A.A. *New Century Bible (Based on the Revised Standard Version): Psalms Volume I*. London: Oliphants, 1972.

ANDERSON, GARY. and LUDWIG, NITA. eds. "Cult of the meta-machine: the coming computerized world." *Epiphany* [special issue] 4 (Fall 1982) pp. 1-136.

ANDERSON, GERALD H., and STRANSKY, THOMAS F., C.S.P., *Mission Trends No., 5: Faith Meets Faith*: (Lively Opinions from four Continents about Christian witness in the encounter with people of other faiths), New York: Paulist Press, 1981.

AQUINAS, THOMAS St., *Summa Theologica* Vol., I., English ed., Westminster: Christian Classics, (1911) 1981.

__________. *Summa Theologica* Vol., II., English ed., Westminster: Christian Classics, (1911) 1981.

__________. *Summa Theologica* Vol., III., English ed., Westminster: Christian Classics, (1911) 1981.

__________. *Summa Theologica* Vol., IV., English ed., Westminster: Christian Classics, (1911) 1981.

__________. *Summa Theologica* Vol., V., English ed., Westminster: Christian Classics, (1911) 1981.

ARNASON, JOHANN P. "Progress and Pluralism: Reflections on Agnes Heller's Theory of History." *Praxis International* 3 (1984) pp. 423-437.

ATHANASIUS, St., *Letter on the Opinion of Dionysius*. Selected and translated by William A. Jurgens, *The Faith of the Early Fathers* Vol., I. Minnesota: the Liturgical Press, 1970, pp. 325-326.

__________. *Discourses Against the Ariens*, selected and translated by William A. Jurgens, *The Faith of the Early Fathers* Vol., I. Minnesota: The Liturgical Press, 1970, pp. 326-334.

__________. *Sermon to the Newly Baptized*, selected and translated by William A. Jurgens, *The Faith of the Early Fathers* Vol., I. Minnesota: The Liturgical Press, 1970, pp. 345-346.

AUGUSTINE OF HIPPO, St., *Against a Discourse of the Arians*, selected and translated by William A. Jurgens, *The Faith of the Early Fathers* Vol., III. (Minnesota: The Liturgical Press, 1970) p. 130-131.

AYKARA, THOMAS A., Ed., *Meeting of Religions: New Orientations and Perspectives*. Bangalore: Dharmaram Publications published for Indian and Inter-Religious Studies, Rome, 1978.

BANERJEE, K.K. "The Meaning of History." in *Logic, Ontology and Action*, edited by H. D. Lewis. Atlantic Highlands Humanities Press, 1982. pp. 1-14.

BAXTER, ANTHONY. "The Term `archetype', and its application to Jesus Christ." *The Hythrop Journal* XXV (1984) pp. 19-38.

BEANE, W. C. *Myth, Cult and Symbols in Sokta Hinduism: A Study of Indian Mother Goddess*. E.J. Brill Leiden, 1977.

BEATTIE, PAUL H. "A Perspective of Mythology." *Religious Humanism* 17 (Autumn 1983) pp. 173-181.

BERLIN, ERIC. "Response to Michael Sugrués: Consciousness in the Marxian Conception of History." *Auslegung* 10 (Spring-Summer 1983) pp. 37-38.

BOYD, ROBIN. *An Introduction to Indian Christian Theology.* Madras: The Christian Literature Society, (1969) 1979.

BRAATEN, CARL E. "The Uniqueness and Universality of Jesus Christ." in *Mission Trends No., 5 Faith Meets Faith: Lively opinions from four*
continents about Christian witness in the encounter with the people *of other Faiths*, Edited by Gerald H. Anderson and Thomas F. Stransky, C.S.P. New York: Paulist Press, 1981. pp.69-89.

BRACKEN, JOSEPH A. sj., *What are they saying about the Trinity?* New York: Paulist Press, 1979.

BRAYBROOKE, M. *The Undiscovered Christ.* Madras: CISRS, CLS, 1973.

BROCKWAY, R.W. "A Critique of Max Müller's Methodology of Mythology." *Journal of Dharma* 2 (October 1977): pp. 368-371.

BROWN, R. E., J. A. FITZMYER and R. E. MURPHY (edts) *The Jerome Biblical Commentary.* London: Geoffrey Chapman, (1969) 1984.

BOS, A. P. "Aristotle on Myth and Philosophy." *Philosophia Reformata* 48 (1983) pp. 1-18.

BULTMANN, RUDOLF. *Jesus Christ and Mythology,* New York: Charles Scribner's Sons, 1958.

CHETHIMATTAM, JOHN B. "Meaning and Scope of Interreligious Dialogue." *Jeevadhara* XI (1981) pp. 319-334.

__________. *Patterns of Indian Thought,* London: Geoffery Chapman; New York: Orbis Books, 1971.

CHIRAPPANATH, A.K. "Mantra and Yantra in Tantra." *Journal of Dharma* 2 (October 1977) pp. 409-426.

CULLMANN, OSCAR. *Christ and Time.* Philadelphia: Westminster Press, 1947.

CULLMANN, OSCAR. *Salvation in History,* New York: Harper & Row, 1967.

CYRIL OF JERUSALEM, St., *Catechetical Lectures*, 13, 33. Selected and translated by William A. Jurgens, *The Faith of the Early Fathers* Vol., I. Minnesota: the Liturgical Press, 1970, pp. 347-371.

DANIÉLOU, J. sj. *The Lord of History: Reflections on the Inner Meaning of History*. London: Longmans, Green and Co Ltd, 1958.

D'ARAGON, JEAN-LOUIS, sj. "The Apocalypse," in R. E. Brown, J. A. Fitzmyer and R. E. Murphy (edts) *The Jerome Biblical Commentary*. London: Geoffrey Chapman, (1969) 1984. 64:1-97.

DASGUPTA, SURENDRANATH, *A History of Indian Philosophy* Vol., I. Cambridge, 1922; reprint, Delhi: Montilal Banarsidass, 1975.

DE LA POTTERIE. "Jesus Christ, plénitude de la vérité." *Studio Missionalia* 33 (1984) pp. 305-324.

DE REINCOURT, AMAURY. *The Soul of India*. (U.K. 1961); Revised ed., New Delhi: Sterling Publishers, 1986.

DHAVAMONY. M. Ed., *Documenta Missionalia 5: Evangelization Dialogue and Development*, (Selected papers of the International Theological Conference: `International Theological Congress on Evangelization' Nagpur India October, 1971. Roma 1972.

"DIGNITATIS HUMANAE" (Declaration on Religious Freedom) in *The Documents of Vatican II*. New Delhi: St Paul Publication, 1966, pp. 554-570.

DUPRÉ LA TOUR, AUGUSIN. "Christologie et Religions non Chrétiennes," *Porche Orient Chrétien*, 36, no., 3-4 (1986) pp. 193-205.

DE SMET, R.V. s.j. "Towards an Indian Christology," *The Clergy Monthly* (Supplement to Vol., XXIX, June 1965): pp. 254-260.

DE URTARAN, Félix. "Muerte de Jesús y definitividad de la revelación cristiana." *Lumen* XXXIII (1984) pp. 193-222.

DUNNE, TAD, sj. "Trinity and History." *Theological Studies* 45 (1984) pp. 139-152.

DUPUIS, J., "The Cosmic Christ in the Early Fathers." *Indian Journal of Theology* (1966) pp. 106-120.

__________. "Christocentrism of Vatican II." *The Clergy Monthly*, 32 (1968) pp. 245-256.

__________. "Nagpur International Theological Conference." *The Clergy Monthly*, 35 (1971) pp. 458-471.

________. "Western Christocentrism and Eastern Pneumatology." *The Clergy Monthly*, 35 (1971) pp. 190-198.

________. "The salvific Value of Non-Christian Religions." In *Evangelization Dialogue and Development*, Dhavamony ed., Roma, 1972, pp. 169-193.

________. "The Cosmic Economy of the Spirit and the Sacred Scriptures of Religious Traditions." In *Research Seminar on Non-Biblical Scriptures*, Amalorpavadass, ed., Bangalore: NBCLC, 1975, pp. 117- 135.

ELIZABETH A. JOHNSON, C.S.J. "The Theological Relevance of the Historical Jesus: A Debate and a Thesis," *The Thomist*, 48 (1984), pp. 1-43.

ELMORE, W. T. *Dravidian God's in Modern Hinduism*. (1913); reprint, New Delhi: Asian Educational Services, 1984.

FALLON, P. sj. "For a True Dialogue Between Christians and Hindus," in *For A Dialogue With Hinduism*. Edt. Secretarius for Non-Christian, Roma, pp. 109-136.

FEDER, P.G. sj. *Messale quotidiano Dei Fedeli*. Roma: Edizione Romane Mame, (1961) 1966.

FITZMYER, J.A. sj. "The Letter to the Philippians," R. Brown, J. A. Fitzmyer and R. E. Murphy (edts) *The Jerome Biblical Commentary*. London: Geoffrey Chapman, 1984, 50:1-27.

FITZMYER, J.A. sj. "The Letter to the Romans," R. Brown, J. A. Fitzmyer and R. E. Murphy (edts) *The Jerome Biblical Commentary*. London: Geoffrey Chapman, 1984, 53:1-140.

FULLER, REGINALD H. "The Historical Jesus Outstanding Issues." *The Thomist* 48 (1984) pp. 368-382.

"GAUDIUM ET SPES" (Pastoral Constitution on the Church in the modern Word), in *The Documents of Vatican II*. New Delhi: St Paul Publication, 1966, pp. 172-280.

GANNE, Pierre. "Who do you Say that I am?" *Cross Currents*, XXXIII (1983) pp. 17-33.

GENEVIEVE, "The Iconography of Kāla-Bhairava." *Journal of Dharma* 2 (October 1977) pp. 427-438.

GREGORY I THE GREAT, POPE St., *Moral Teachings Drawn from Job*, selected and translated by William A. Jurgens, *The Faith of the Early Fathers* Vol., III. Minnesota the Liturgical Press, 1970) pp. 313-318.

GRIFFITHS, BEDE. *The Cosmic Revelation*. Bangalore: Asian Trading Corporation, (1983) 1985.

__________. *The Marriage of East and West*. London: Collins Fount Paperbacks, (1982) 1983.

__________. *Return To The Centre*. London: Collins Fount Paperbacks, (1976) 1984.

GRILLMEIER, ALOYS sj. *Christ in Christian Tradition, Vol., 1: From the Apostolic Age to Chalcedon (AD 451)*. Great Britain: A.R.Mowbray & Co. Limited, (1965); revised ed., 1975.

__________. *Christ in Christian Tradition, Vol., 2: From the Council of Chalcedon (451) to Gregory the Great (590-604), Part One: Reception and Contradiction, The development of the discussion about Chalcedon from 451 to the beginning of the reign of Justinian*. London & Oxford: A.R.Mowbray & Co. Limited, 1987.

HAAG, HERBERT. "`Son of God' in the Language and Thinking of the Old Testament." *Concilium* 153 (3/1982) pp. 31-36.

HACKER, PAUL. "Religiöse Toleranz und Intoleranz im Hinduismus." in *Kleine Schriften*, pp. 376ff.

HAENCHEN, E. *The Acts of the Apostles* (Oxford, 1971).

HELFER, J. "Brahma Sútras," in *Abingdon Dictionary of Living Religions*, Gen. Ed. Keith Crim. Tennessee: Abingdon, 1981.

HEMPEL, J. "Psalms, Book of," in *The Interpreter's Dictionary of the Bible*, Vol., 3, edited by George Arthur Buttrick. Nashville (USA): Abingdon Press, (1962) 1982, pp. 942-958.

HILL, WILLIAM. J., O.P. "The History of God." *Theological Studies* 45 (1984) pp. 320-333.

HOBSBAWN, ERIC J. "Karl Marx et l'historie." *Diogéne*, no., 125 (1984) pp. 108-121.

HOOKER, ROGER. "Hindu Impressions of Christ and Christianity," in *Mission Trends No., 5 Faith Meets Faith: Lively opinions from four continents about Christian witness in the encounter with the people of other Faiths*, Edited by Gerald H. Anderson and Thomas F. Stransky, C.S.P. New York: Paulist Press, 1981. pp.258-263.

HOY, DAVID COUZENS. *The Critical Circle. Literature and History in Contemporary Hermeneutics.* Berkeley: University of California Press, 1978.

HUME, ROBERT ERNST. *The Thirteen Principal Upanishads.* (Translated from the Sanskrit), New Delhi: Oxford University Press, (1921) 1984.

HÜNERMANN, P. "Geschichte der Christologie-Geschicte Jesu Christi mit den Menschen?" *Theologische Quartals Schrift* 164 (1984) pp. 102-120.

ILLICKAMURY, CYPRIAN. *The Lordship of Jesus Christ: over the World and the Church: the Christological Witness of the Pastoral Constitution "Gaudium et Spes".* Bangalore: ATC, 1980.

IRENAEUS, St. *Adversus haereses*, selected and translated by William A. Jurgens, *The Faith of the Early Fathers* Vol., I. Minnesota: The Liturgical Press, 1970, pp. 84-104.

JACOBS, JONATHAN. "The Idea of Personal History." *International Philosophical Quarterly* XXIV (June 1984) pp. 179-189.

JENNI, E. "Messiah, Jewish" in *The Interpreter's Dictionary of the Bible*, Vol., 3, edited by George Arthur Buttrick. Nashville (USA): Abingdon Press, (1962) 1982, pp. 360-365.

JOHN DAMASCENE, St., *The Source of Knowledge*, selected and translated by William A. Jurgens, *The Faith of the Early Fathers* Vol., III. Minnesota: the Liturgical Press, 1970, p. 331-344.

JOHNSON, ELIZABETH A., C.S.J. "Theological Relevance of the Historical Jesus: A Debate and a Thesis." *The Thomist* 48 (January 1984) pp. 1-43.

JURGENS, WILLIAM A. Selected and translated, *The Faith of the Early Fathers* Vol., I. Minnesota: the Liturgical Press, 1970.

JURGENS, WILLIAM A. Selected and translated, *The Faith of the Early Fathers* Vol., II. Minnesota: Liturgical Press, 1979.

JURGENS, WILLIAM A. (Selected and translated) *The Faith of the Early Fathers* Vol., III. Minnesota: Liturgical Press, 1979.

JUSTIN THE MARTYR, St. *First Apology* in W.A. Jurgens, Selected and translated *The Faith of the Early Fathers* Vol., I. Minnesota: Liturgical Press, 1970, pp. 50-57.

__________. *Second Apology* in W.A. Jurgens, selected and translated *The Faith of the Early Fathers* Vol., I. Minnesota: Liturgical Press, 1970, p. 57.

KADICHEENI, PAUL. "Religious Pluralism and the Uniqueness of Christ." (chronicle). *Journal of Dharma* 3 (January-March 1978) pp. 102-105.

KAṬHA UPANISHAD. Translated by R.E. Hume, *The Thirteen Principal Upanishads*. New Delhi: Oxford University Press, 1984, pp. 341-361.

KÄSEMANN, ERNST. *Commentary on Romans*. Great Britain: SCM Press, 1980.

KASPER, WALTER. *Jesus The Christ*, London: Burns & Oates; New York: Paulist Press, 1981.

__________. *The God of Jesus Christ*. New York: The Crossroad Publishing Company, 1988.

KEJR, VACLAV. "The Christ of the Future." *Communino Viatorum* No 1&2 (1984) pp. 1-5.

KHODR, GEORGES. "The Economy of the Holy Spirit." in *Mission Trends No., 5 Faith Meets Faith: Lively opinions from four continents about Christian witness in the encounter with the people of other Faiths*, edited by Gerald H. Anderson and Thomas F. Stransky, C.S.P. New York: Paulist Press, 1981. pp. 36-49.

KLANCK J.H., O.F.M. "Die Sakramente und der historische Jesus." *Wissenschaft Und Weisheit*, 47 (1984) pp. 1-11.

KOCHUMUTTOM, T. *Comparative Theology: Christian Thinking and Spirituality in Indian Perspective*. Bangalore: Dharmaram Publications, 1985.

KRASS, A.L., "Proclaiming the Inner Christ of Hinduism: An Interview with Paul Sudhakar." in *Mission Trends No., 5 Faith Meets Faith: Lively opinions from four continents about Christian witness in the encounter with the people of other Faiths*, Edited by Gerald H. Anderson and Thomas F. Stransky, C.S.P. New York: Paulist Press,

1981, pp.264-270.

KÜNG, HANS. "The World Religions in God's Plan of Salvation." in *Christian Revelation and World Religions*, ed. J. Neuner. London: Burns and Oates, 1967. pp. 67-122.

KÜNG, HANS, VAN ESS, J.; VON STIETENCRON, H.; and BECHERT, H. *Christentum und Welt-Religionen. Hinführung zum Dialog mit Islam, Hinduismus und Buddhismus.* München Zürich: Piper, 1984.

LASH, NICHOLAS. "`Son of God`: Reflections on a Metaphor." *Concilium* 153 (3/1982) pp. 11-16.

LECLERCQ, J. "Le Christ - moine." *Studia Missionalia* 33 (1984) pp. 403-411.

LEO THE GREAT, POPE St., *The Tome of Leo: Letter of Pope Leo I To Flavian, Bishop of Constantinople.* June 13, 449 A.D. 28, 5. selected and translated by William A. Jurgens, *The Faith of the Early Fathers* Vol., III. Minnesota: the Liturgical Press, 1970, pp. 270-271.

LÉVI-STRAUSS, C. *La pensée sauvage.* Paris: Plon, 1962.

LOHSE, EDUARD. *Colossians and Philemon: A Commentary on the Epistle to the Colossians and to Philemon.* Translated by William R. Poehlmann and Robert J. Karris. Edited by Helmut Koester. Philadelphia: Fortress Press, 1971; Third Printing, 1982.

LOURDUSAMY, D. SIMON, "Meeting of Religions I - Indian Orientations," (Keynote address at the inauguration of the Centre for Indian and Inter-Religious Studies in Rome on 15th September, 1977) in *Meeting of Religions: New Orientations and Perspectives*, edt. Thomas, A. Aykara, (Bangalore: Dharmaram Publications published for Indian and Inter-Religious Studies, Rome, 1978) pp. 7-24.

LYONS, J.A. *The Cosmic Christ in Origen and Teilhard de Chardin: A Comparative Study.* Oxford University Press, 1982.

MAITRI UPANISHAD, Translated by R.E. Hume, *The Thirteen Principal Upanishads.* New Delhi: Oxford University Press, 1984, pp. 412-458.

MANICKAM, T.M. "Editorial." *Journal of Dharma* 2 (October 1977): pp. 365-367.

_______. "The `Myth of Origin', Aryan and Hebrew. A comparative interpretation." *Journal of Dharma* 2 (October 1977) pp. 397-409.

McDERMOTT, BRIAN. "Jesus Christ in Today's Faith and Theology." *Concilium* 153 (3/1982) pp. 3-10.

McDONALD, "The Kerygmatic Christology of Rudolf Bultmann," in *Christ the Lord: Studies in Christology. Presented to Donald Guthrie*, H.H.Rowdon, ed., Leiscester: Inter-Versity Press, 1982, pp. 311- 325.

MENACHERRY, CHERIYAN. *An Indian Philosophical Approach to the Personality of Jesus Christ*. Roma: Urbaniana University Press, 1986.

_______. "Patriarchal Approaches towards 'World Religions'." *Jeevadhara* XIV (March 1984) pp. 95-108.

MÜHLEN, HERIBERT. *Der Heilige Geist als Person*. Münster: Münsterliche Beitrag zur Theologie, 2nd ed., 1967.

MURPHY, JOHN W. "Foucault's Ground of History." *International Philosophical Quarterly* XXIV (1984) pp. 189-196.

NEUNER, J. *Christian Revelation and World Religions*. London: Burns and Oates, 1967.

NEUNER, J., sj. & J. DUPUIS sj., Ed., *The Christian Faith: in the Doctrinal Documents of the Catholic Church*. Bangalore: Theological Publication in India, 1973; third edition 1978.

NEWBIGIN, LESSLIE. "The Gospel Among Religions." in *Mission Trends No., 5 Faith Meets Faith: Lively opinions from four continents about Christian witness in the encounter with the people of other Faiths*, edited by Gerald H. Anderson and Thomas F. Stransky, C.S.P. New York: Paulist Press, 1981. pp. 3-19.

"NOSTRA AETATE" (Declaration on the Relation of the Church to Non- Christian Religions), in *The Documents of Vatican II*. New Delhi: St Paul Publication, 1966, pp. 548-553.

OLSON, ALAN., ed. *Myth, Symbol and Reality*. Notre Dame: University of Notre Dame Press, 1980.

ORIGEN, *De pincipiis*. Selected and translated by William A. Jurgens, *The Faith of the Early Fathers* Vol., I. Minnesota: The

Liturgical Press, 1970, pp. 190-200.

PANNENBERG, W., ed. *Revelation as History*. 2nd ed. London: Sheed and Ward, 1979.

__________. "Dogmatic Thesis on the Doctrine of Revelation," in *Revelation as History*, W. Pannenberg, ed., 2nd ed., London: Sheed and Ward, 1979, pp. 123-158.

PATRAPANKAL, JOSEPH. *Service and Salvation*, ed., Bangalore: Theological Publications in India, 1973.

PIERIS, ALOYSIUS. "Speaking of the Son of God in Non-Christian Cultures, e.g., in Asia." *Concilium* 153 (3/1982) pp. 65-70.

PIGGOTT, S. *Prehistoric India*, Harmondsworth, Middlesex, 1950.

QUASTEN, JOHANNES. *Patrology* Vo. I: *The beginnings of Patristic Literature. From the Apostles Creed to Irenaeus*, Westminster: Christian Classics, Inc., (1950) 1984.

__________. *Patrology* Vo. II: *The Ante-Nicene Literatur After Irenaeus*, Westminster: Christian Classics, Inc., (1950) 1984.

RAMAN, N.S.S. "The Language of Myth in Religion." *Journal of Dharma* 2 (October 1977) pp. 372-381.

RAHNER, KARL. "The eternal significance of the humanity of Jesus for our relationship with God." in *Theological Investigations, Vol., 3: Theology of the Spiritual Life*. Translated by Karl-H. and Boniface Kruger. London: Darton Longman & Todd, (1967) 1987, pp. 35-46.

__________. "On the Theology of the Incarnation," in *Theological Investigations, Vol., 4: More Recent Writings*. Translated by Kelvin Smith. London: Darton, Longman & Todd, (1966) 1987, pp. 105-120.

__________. "Theology of the Symbol," in *Theological Investigations, Vol., 4: More Recent Writings*, Translated by Kelvin Smith. London: Darton, Longman & Todd, (1966) 1987, pp. 221-252.

__________. "Christianity and the Non-Christian Religions." in *Theological Investigation, Vol., 5: Later Writings*. Translated by Karl H. Kruger. London: Darton, Longman & Todd, (1966) 1984. pp. 115-134.

__________. "The Individual and the Church: Anonymous Christians," *Theological Investigations, Vol., 6: Concerning Vatican*

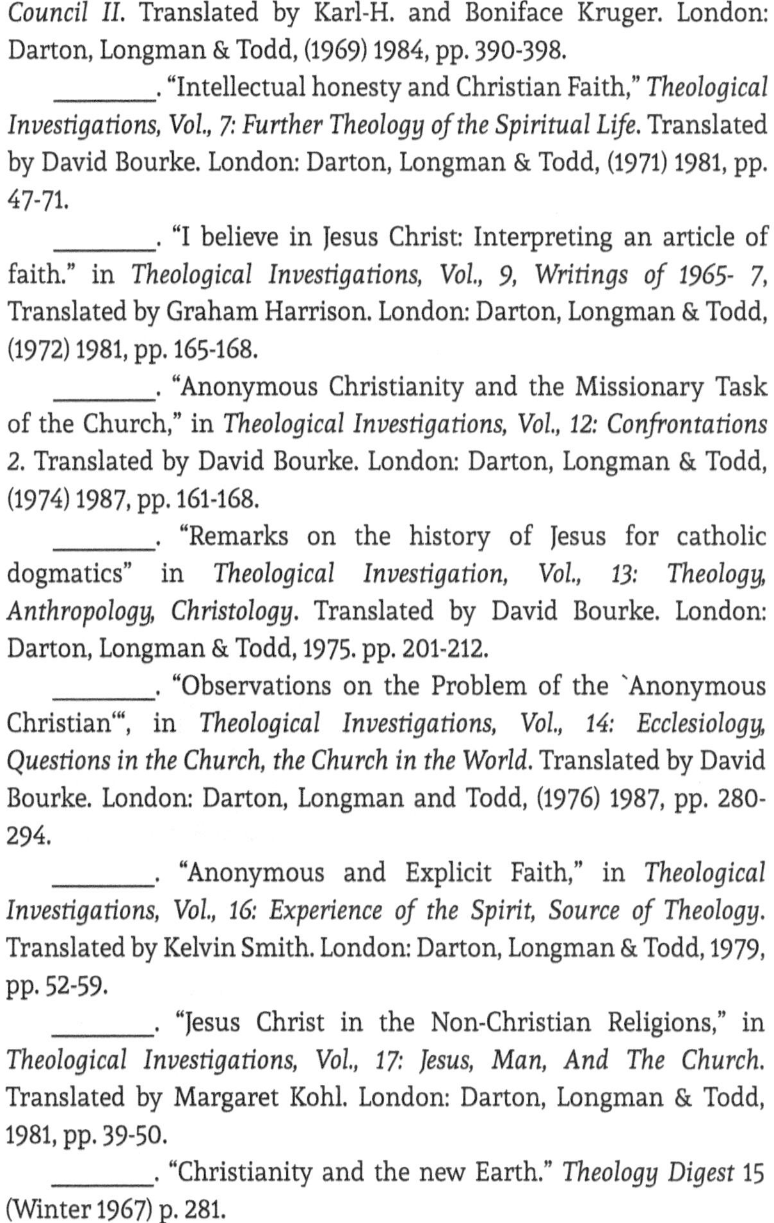

Council II. Translated by Karl-H. and Boniface Kruger. London: Darton, Longman & Todd, (1969) 1984, pp. 390-398.

_________. "Intellectual honesty and Christian Faith," *Theological Investigations, Vol., 7: Further Theology of the Spiritual Life*. Translated by David Bourke. London: Darton, Longman & Todd, (1971) 1981, pp. 47-71.

_________. "I believe in Jesus Christ: Interpreting an article of faith." in *Theological Investigations, Vol., 9, Writings of 1965- 7*, Translated by Graham Harrison. London: Darton, Longman & Todd, (1972) 1981, pp. 165-168.

_________. "Anonymous Christianity and the Missionary Task of the Church," in *Theological Investigations, Vol., 12: Confrontations 2*. Translated by David Bourke. London: Darton, Longman & Todd, (1974) 1987, pp. 161-168.

_________. "Remarks on the history of Jesus for catholic dogmatics" in *Theological Investigation, Vol., 13: Theology, Anthropology, Christology*. Translated by David Bourke. London: Darton, Longman & Todd, 1975. pp. 201-212.

_________. "Observations on the Problem of the `Anonymous Christian'", in *Theological Investigations, Vol., 14: Ecclesiology, Questions in the Church, the Church in the World*. Translated by David Bourke. London: Darton, Longman and Todd, (1976) 1987, pp. 280-294.

_________. "Anonymous and Explicit Faith," in *Theological Investigations, Vol., 16: Experience of the Spirit, Source of Theology*. Translated by Kelvin Smith. London: Darton, Longman & Todd, 1979, pp. 52-59.

_________. "Jesus Christ in the Non-Christian Religions," in *Theological Investigations, Vol., 17: Jesus, Man, And The Church*. Translated by Margaret Kohl. London: Darton, Longman & Todd, 1981, pp. 39-50.

_________. "Christianity and the new Earth." *Theology Digest* 15 (Winter 1967) p. 281.

_________. Ed., *Encyclopedia of Theology: A Concise Sacramentum Mundi*. London: Burns & Oates, (1975) 1981.

________. "Christology Today," in *Concilium: Religion in the Eighties: Jesus, Son of God?* Edts, Edward Schillebeeckx and Johannes-Baptist Metz. Edinburgh: T. & T. Clark LTD; New York: The Seabury Press, 1982, pp. 73-77.

________. "Jesus Christ." in *Foundations of Christian Faith: An Introduction to the idea of Christianity.* Translated by William V. Dych. (German edition, Freiburg: Verlag Herder, 1976) New York: Crossroad, (1978) 1984. pp. 176-321.

RAULET, GE'RARD. "La Fin De La `Raison Dans L'Histoire'." *Dialogue* 22 (December 1983) pp. 631-646.

REESE, WILLIAM L. *Dictionary of Philosophy and Religion: Eastern and Western Thought.* New Jersey: Humanity press Inc., and Sussex: The Harvester Press Limited, 1980.

RICOEUR, PAUL. *The Reality of the Historical Past.* Milwankee Marquette Uni. Press, 1984.

[RJ.], "Christology and non-Christian religions," observations of "Christologie et Religions non Chrétiennes," *Porche Orient Chrétien*, 36, no., 3-4 (1986) pp. 193-205, by Augusin Dupré la Tour, in *Theology Digest*, 35, (Summer 1988), pp. 103-106.

ROBERTS, JOY H. "Two Kinds of Knowledge on Croce's Philosophy of History." *International Studies in Philosophy* 14 (Spring 1982) pp. 35-48.

ROTENSTREICH, NATHAN. "Universalism and Particularism in History." *Review of Metaphysics* 37 (Sept. 1983) pp. 21-36.

ROSSANO, PIETRO. "Christ's Lordship and Religious Pluralism." in *Mission Trends No., 5, Faith Meets Faith: Lively opinions from four continents about Christian witness in the encounter with the people of other Faiths,* Edited by Gerald H. Anderson and Thomas F. Stransky, C.S.P. New York: Paulist Press, 1981, pp.21-35.

SACNTON, THOMAS A. "Planet of the Year: What on earth are we doing," *Time: Planet of the Year, Endangered Earth,* (January 2, 1989) pp. 13-18.

SCHEFFCZYK, LEO. "Christology in the Context of Experience: On the Interpretation of Christ by E. Schillebeeckx." *The Thomist* 48 (1984) pp. 383-408.

SCHILLEBEECKX, Edward. *Jesus: An Experiment in Christology.* London: William Collins Sons & Co Ltd., and New York: The Seabury Press, Inc., 1979; London: Fount Paperbacks, 1983.

SCHILLEBEECKX, EDWARD AND METZ, JOHANNES-BAPTIST. "Jesus as Son of God" (Editorial). *Concilium* 153 (3/1982) pp. vii-ix.

SCHMITHALS, WALTER. *An Introduction to the theology of Rudolf Bultmann*, Translated by John Bowden, London: SCM Press Ltd, 1967.

SECRETARIATUS PRO NON CHRISTIANS, *For a Dialogue with Hinduism.* Milano, Roma: Editrice Anchora, n.d.

SEIFERT, JOSEPH. "Truth and History: Noumenal Phenomenology." *Diotima* 11 (1983) pp. 160-183.

SHARMA, ARVIND. "The Lost Veda and the Unknown Christ," in *The Indian Journal of Theology* 30, no., 1 (1981) pp. 24-28.

SOBRINO, JON. "A Crucified People's Faith in the Son of God." *Concilium* 153 (3/1982) pp. 23-28.

SPLETT, JÖRG. "Symbol." in K Rahner, ed. *Encyclopedia of Theology: A Concise Sacramentum Mundi.* London: Burns & Oates, (1975) 1981. pp. 1654-1657.

STEVENSON, W.T. *History as Myth.* New York: Seabury Press, 1969.

__________. "History as Myth: Some Implications for History and Theology." *Cross Currents* (Winter 1970) pp. 15-28.

STUART - FOX, MARTIN. "On The Theory of History and its Context of Discovery." *Philosophy of the Social Sciences* 13 (December 1983) pp. 401-424.

STUTLEY, MARGARET and JAMES, *A Dictionary of Hinduism: Its Mythology, Folklore and Development 1500 B.C.-A.D. 1500.* Bombay: Allied Publishers, 1977.

SURIN, KENNETH. "Revelation, Salvation, The Uniqueness of Christ And Other Religions." *Religious Studies* 19 (September 1983) pp. 323-344.

SWAMI CHIDBHAVANANDA, (commented) *The Bhagavad Gita.* Tamil Nadu: Sri Ramakrishna Tapovanam, 1979.

SWAMI KRISHNANANDA, *A Short History of Religious and Philosophic Thought in India.* India: The Divine Life Society, 1970.

TAYLOR, JOHN V. "The Theological Basis of Interfaith Dialogue," in *Mission Trends No., 5, Faith Meets Faith: Lively opinions from four continents about Christian witness in the encounter with the people of other Faiths*, Edited by Gerald H. Anderson and Thomas F. Stransky, C.S.P. New York: Paulist Press, 1981, pp. 93-110.

TAYSOR, STEVENSON, W. "History as Myth: Some Implications for History and Theology." *Cross Currents* XX (Winter, 1970) pp. 15-28.

TEASDALE, WAYNE. "Bede Griffiths and the Uniqueness of Christianity." *Communio* 11 (1984) pp. 177-185.

THE ORGANIZING COMMITTEE ALL INDIA SEMINAR. *All India Seminar on the Church in India Today, Bangalore, May 15-25, 1969, Orientation Papers.* New Delhi: The Organizing Committee C.B.C.I. Centre, 1969.

THILS, G. *Transcendence ou? Incarnation?*, Louvain, 1950.

VAN IERSEL, BAS. "`Son of God' in the New Testament." *Concilium* 153 (3/1982) pp. 37-48.

VAN BAVEL, TARSICIUS, "Chalcedon: Then and Now," in *Concilium: Religion in the Eighties: Jesus, Son of God?* Edts Edward Schillebeeckx and Johannes-Baptist Metz. Edinburgh: T. & T. Clark LTD; New York: The Seabury Press, 1982, pp. 55-62.

VAWTER, BRUCE, cm., "The Gospel According to John," in *Jerom Biblical Commentary*, edts, Brown, R. E., J. A. Fitzmyer and R. E. Murphy, (London: Geoffrey Chapman, [1969] 1984), 63:1-186.

VINCENT OF LERINS, St., *Notebooks*, selected and translated by William A. Jurgens, *The Faith of the Early Fathers* Vol., III. Minnesota: the Liturgical Press, 1970, pp. 261-266.

VITSAXIS, VASSILIS G. *Hindu Epics, Myths and Legends in Popular Illustrations.* Oxford: Oxford University Press, 1977; reprint, New Delhi: Oxford University Press, 1984.

VON LEYDEN, WOLFGANG. "Categories of Historical Understanding." *History and Theory* 23 (1984) pp. 53-77.

WALKER, IAN. "Professor Wiles on Historical Christology." *New Blackfriars* 60 (1979) pp. 52-61.

WAINWRIGHT, GEOFFREY. "`Son of God' in Liturgical Doxologies." *Concilium* 153 (3/1982) pp. 49-54.

WIEDERKEHR, DIETRICH. "'Son of God' and 'Sons of God': The Social Relevance of the Christological Title." *Concilium* 153 (3/1982) pp. 17-22.

WILSON, TOM. Christian Responses to Five Views of the Bhagavad Gita: Entry into Dialogue, Newcastle upon Tyne: Cambridge Scholars Publishing, 2021

WOLFSON, H.A. *The Philosophy of the Church Fathers*. Vol., I., Cambridge, Mass: Harvard University Press, 2nd. ed., 1964.

www.ingramcontent.com/pod-product-compliance
Lightning Source LLC
Chambersburg PA
CBHW031136130726

47988CB00006B/2391